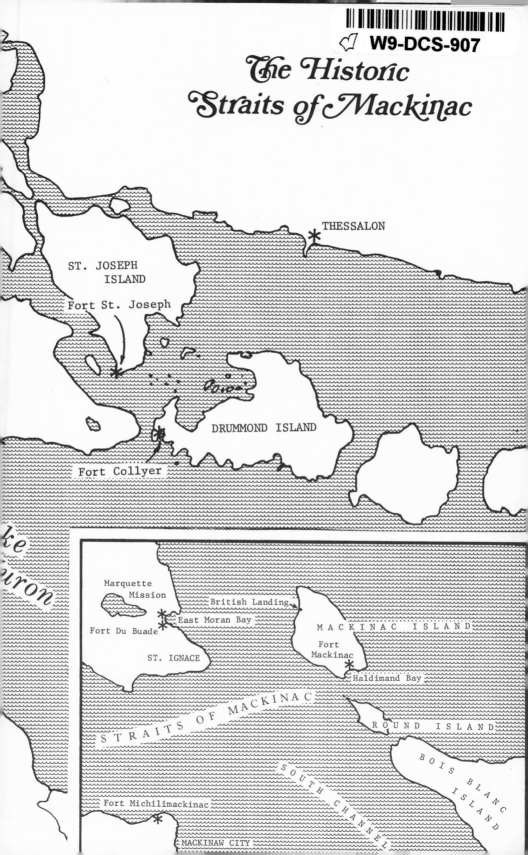

The Historic Straits of Mackinac

THESSALON

ST. JOSEPH
ISLAND

Fort St. Joseph

DRUMMOND ISLAND

Fort Collyer

Lake Huron

Marquette
Mission

British Landing

Fort Du Buade

East Moran Bay

MACKINAC ISLAND

ST. IGNACE

Fort
Mackinac

Haldimand Bay

STRAITS OF MACKINAC

ROUND ISLAND

BOIS BLANC ISLAND

SOUTH CHANNEL

Fort Michilimackinac

MACKINAW CITY

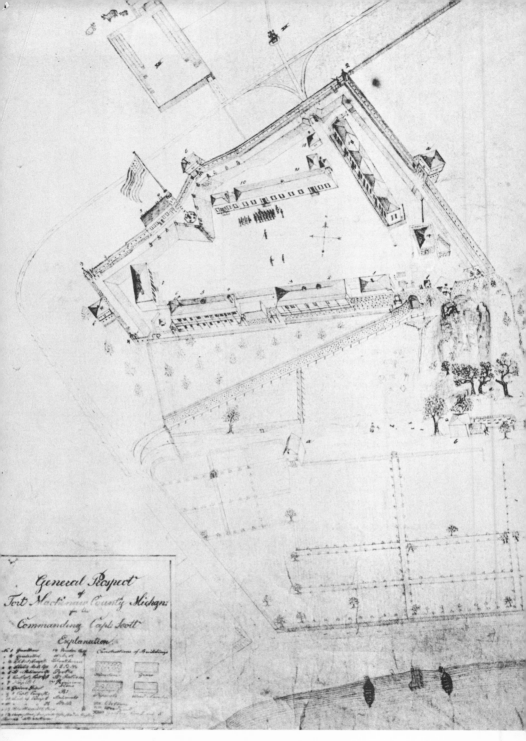

Private W. Brenschutz's sketch of Fort Mackinac in 1842. Courtesy—William L. Clements Library, University of Michigan.

REVEILLE TILL TAPS
SOLDIER LIFE AT FORT MACKINAC
1780 - 1895

by

Keith R. Widder

Illustrated by

Dirk Gringhuis

Mackinac State Historic Parks

Mackinac Island, Michigan

Copyright 1972   15,000 copies
1994   4,000 copies

AN ACT,

ESTABLISHING

RULES and ARTICLES

FOR THE

Government of the Armies

OF THE

UNITED STATES ;

WITH THE

Regulations of the War Department

RESPECTING THE SAME.

———

TO WHICH ARE ADDED,

The several Laws relative to the ARMY; the MILITIA
when in actual service; VOLUNTEERS ; RANGERS;
ORDNANCE DEPARTMENT, and the QUARTER MAS-
TER'S and COMMISSARY GENERAL'S Departments.

———

ALBANY:

PRINTED BY WEBSTERS AND SKINNERS:

....

1812.

Title page of early ARMY REGULATIONS *which determined how soldiers lived at Fort Mackinac.*

CONTENTS

ILLUSTRATIONS

INTRODUCTION

In 1895 the United States Army abandoned Fort Mackinac. This marked the end of over two centuries of military activity in the Straits of Mackinac. The French first sent soldiers to Michilimackinac, then located in modern St. Ignace in the late seventeenth century. The English victory over France in the French and Indian War resulted in the arrival of British troops at Fort Michilimackinac then situated on the south side of the straits.

From 1761 until 1895 a number of distant events took place that had serious ramifications at Mackinac. Five years after the American Revolution broke out in 1775 the British decided to move their garrison to Mackinac Island. Even though the Americans won the war, they did not get control of Fort Mackinac until 1796. This was accomplished through a treaty negotiated by John Jay with the British the year before. The American army was present at Mackinac for sixteen years until the British captured the fort during the War of 1812. Fortunately for the United States the Treaty of Ghent in 1815 returned the post to the Americans.

Although the United States maintained control of Fort Mackinac for the next eighty years it was not always garrisoned by regular army troops. Several times war required the service of the men at Mackinac. Due to the manpower needs generated by Indian Wars, the post was abandoned most of the time from June, 1837 to May, 1840 and from September, 1856 to June, 1858. During the Mexican War in May, 1847 the garrison was ordered to serve in the conflict. It was not until November, 1848 that the Fourth Infantry reoccupied the fort. Likewise the Civil War created a great demand for men to fight the Confederate Army. In early 1861 the Second Artillery left the post and no regular unit returned until 1867. For part of the times that the fort was vacated, units of the Michigan Volunteers were present.

Following the Civil War, Fort Mackinac had little military significance. However in 1875 the United States Congress created Mackinac Island National Park. For years the soldiers had cared for the military reservation on the island, and now they made the park accessible to summer visitors. In 1895 when the soldiers left the fort, Congress turned the park over to the State of Michigan to be used as its first state park.

Throughout Fort Mackinac's 115 year history the soldiers stationed there were part of Mackinac Island society. To their good fortune a sizable and active community thrived just several hundred yards below the fort. The village of Mackinac Island was a fur trade center throughout the last two decades of the eighteenth and the first one-third of the nineteenth centuries. After that, fishing was the prime activity for a few decades, and by 1875 thousands of tourists visited the island during the summer months. This community played an integral part in most of the soldiers' lives. It was here where they played, worshipped, got drunk, got into trouble, met girls, and visited with civilians.

Although the village was important, these men were soldiers, and the wishes and commands of the army took precedence over their personal desires. They drilled, cut firewood, built fort buildings, walked their posts, policed the fort, and performed countless other activities. The army made great demands upon its men and paid them little in return, but it did provide for their basic bodily needs. Food was procured, prepared, and served to the men. A post surgeon stationed at the fort cared for the sick and injured. To satisfy some intellectual curiosities, books and periodicals were purchased for the men's use. Since only a few men had wives and children, they spent much time entertaining each other playing cards and assorted games, among other recreational activities.

Except for a few years immediately after the War of 1812, the number of men stationed at the fort was usually under one hundred, often only forty or fifty. Men generally spent several years at the garrison. This gave them ample time to get to know the community and the island very well.

A study of soldier life at Fort Mackinac reveals that the men endured some severe hardships. Mackinac Island was isolated and very cold, yet life was not as bad as one might think. It must be remembered that these men lived in the late eighteeneth or the nineteenth century, not in the twentieth century. A man might feel quite lonely and depressed on a bitter January evening, but he had much more company than many folks living in rural regions of Ohio, Indiana, New York, or any remote area in the northern United States. A soldier at the fort had his comrades around him and a village nearby.

Soldiers were not the only people who had to cut firewood, build roads, or carry water. Countless civilians performed similar functions to survive. Throughout most of Fort Mackinac's history, much of America was a frontier. To be sure, by 1895 the American frontier had come to a close, but during the preceeding one hundred years, many persons made great sacrifices to clear land, build settlements, and develop the country's resources. The soldiers at Mackinac were called upon to do their part, too. They did not always do so willingly.

One must also be careful not to judge or evaluate nineteenth-century life by twentieth-century standards. For those of us who heat our homes by adjusting a thermostat, chopping firewood in ten degree weather seems incredibly harsh. Likewise, our dependence on such conveniences as running water, indoor plumbing, television, freezers, and electric stoves makes it difficult for us to understand the need to undertake laborious procedures to fulfill our most basic needs. Yet, hard physical labor often in a severe environment was necessary for one to survive.

So much for that; let us proceed with the story of the men who made Fort Mackinac a place worth remembering.

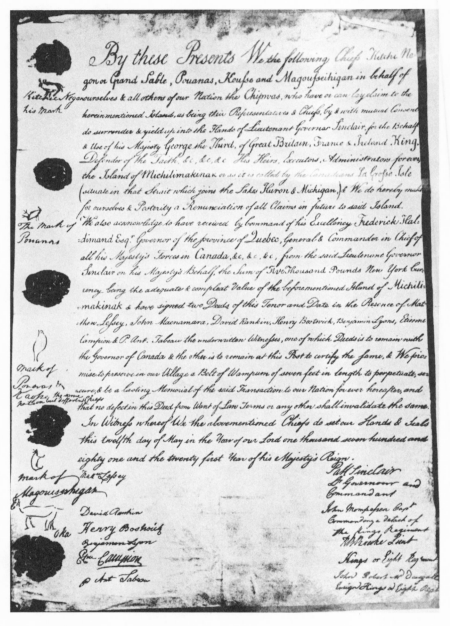

Treaty signed by Chippewa chiefs and Lieutenant Governor Patrick Sinclair ceding Mackinac Island to Great Britain. Courtesy — William L. Clements Library, University of Michigan.

I.
THE
BEGINNINGS

Military life began on Mackinac Island during the winter of 1779-1780. Those first soldiers had traveled several thousand miles from Great Britain to serve their King in the remote place called Michilimackinac. Yet they were not the first soldiers to serve in the Straits area. Despite its great distance from Europe, Europeans had been in this wild country over a century and a half.

The first white intruders in the Great Lakes region were from France. These hardy Frenchmen came to explore the wilderness and to discover the riches it held. Jean Nicolet paddled past Mackinac Island in 1634 on his way to Green Bay and his famous meeting with the Indians. Many others followed.

The French thrust into the heart of this new world in search of fur. This enterprise brought the *voyageurs* and *coureurs de bois* into direct contact with the Indians. These adventurous Frenchmen spent years living among the natives, learning their language and customs and sometimes marrying their women. While the French learned much about the Indians' way of life, they also brought about tremendous changes in Indian society. As the Indian became accustomed to using the white man's products which he acquired in trade, he became dependent upon them. Blankets, knives, kettles, trinkets, and rum soon became necessities, and the only way the native could survive was to acquire more furs to trade.

Not all Frenchmen viewed the North American inhabitants as a means of acquiring wealth. Dedicated priests sought to convert them to the Roman Catholic faith. As early as 1641 the Jesuit Fathers Isaac Jogues

1

and Charles Raymboult preached to the Chippewas of Sault Ste. Marie. In 1670 Fathers Claude Dablon and Jacques Marquette visited Mackinac Island, and the next year Marquette established a mission to the Huron and Ottawa tribes at St. Ignace. This marked the beginning of the white man's attempt to control the Straits of Mackinac.

A primary concern of the French during the later part of the seventeenth and early eighteenth centuries was the increasing strength and influence of Great Britain. While this rivalry was world wide in scope, it manifested itself overtly in the struggle for control of the North American fur trade and the interior of the continent. As a result, the French in 1689 built Fort DuBuade at St. Ignace, which was abandoned a few years later. However, the continuing British threat necessitated the construction of Fort Michilimackinac about 1715 on the south side of the Straits.

Fort Michilimackinac served as a center for French fur traders, where they outfitted themselves for their voyages into the wilderness further west. All goods were transported in birch canoes and plank batteaux, as the water routes were the only means of communications. In addition a few French troops and militia protected the King's interest in this remote land.

Ultimately the control of Michilimackinac was determined by the outcome of the French and Indian War between 1754 and 1763. Britain won and forced France to abandon her outposts, including Michilimackinac. Consequently, the Red Ensign replaced the Fleur de Lis over the Straits in 1761 without a shot being fired upon the garrison. Since Britain guaranteed the French inhabitants their property rights and the freedom to practice their Roman Catholic faith, many Frenchmen remained at Michilimackinac as fur traders.

For the next twenty years the fort continued its important role in the fur trade with a sizable community consisting of approximately one hundred buildings growing up east of the stockade. The Indians supplied furs, fish, corn, and game in exchange for trade goods and rum. The neighboring tribes became as dependent upon the British as they had been previously on the French.

Meanwhile forces were unleashed that meant serious trouble for the British. Colonists in the East resisted political and economic measures enacted by the British government, and by 1775 these actions resulted in open rebellion against the mother country. The early battles of the American Revolution were fought hundreds of miles from Michilimackinac. However, in 1778 the alarming successes of a young Virginian, George Rogers Clark, sent shock waves all the way to the Straits. His conquests of Cahokia, Kaskaskia, and Vincennes, and the capture of Governor Henry Hamilton convinced the British commander, Lieutenant Governor Patrick Sinclair, who had arrived in October, 1779, that

Michilimackinac would be virtually defenseless against an American attack. Sinclair feared that the rebels might send an expedition up Lake Michigan from the Illinois country, and he knew that Michilimackinac's palisades would be defenseless against American cannon. Hence he quickly decided to move the installation to more defensible Mackinac Island.

Sinclair and several artisans examined the natural features and resources of the island in early October, 1779, and found it to be an ideal location. A fine natural harbor on the island's south end could accommodate sailing vessels. Several hundred feet from the shore a steep hill rose 150 feet above the water level. A fortification constructed atop this elevation would be safe from artillery fire. Timber, stone, and clay to build a new fort were present in abundance. Finally, the soil would support vegetation necessary for the soldiers' diet.

Convinced that the island offered a sanctuary for his garrison, Sinclair formulated plans to move. He wanted to build a fort on the hill, a wharf, and store houses on the lower ground. The sizable area near the harbor would be the site of a village for the traders and civilians. These designs were forwarded to his superiors in Quebec. Without waiting for the approval of General Frederick Haldimand, Governor of Quebec, Sinclair moved quickly to solidify his position. First, he beefed up the defenses at Michilimackinac by strengthening the palisades. Then all traders and servants were enrolled in the militia to increase their awareness of possible danger.

Mural painted by Dirk Gringhuis depicting British soldiers and French Canadians constructing Fort Mackinac.

That winter British troops started building Fort Mackinac, beginning 115 years of soldier life on Mackinac Island. Five soldiers accompanied by a carpenter built a wharf in Haldimand Bay. The King's vessels docked here for the winter with their crews adding more manpower for the construction work. Four acres of land on the upper ground were cleared and sixty cords of firewood prepared in the process. The soldiers squared timbers, cut poles, fashioned pickets, and erected a blockhouse near the water to provide shelter from the bitter winter elements. By February, Sinclair's men began quarrying stone and burning lime for the masonry fort he planned.

During the next couple of years, the British troops erected the walls and the first set of buildings that comprised Fort Mackinac. They constructed a barracks, well, stone powder magazine, guardhouse, King's storehouse and the foundation of the officers' stone quarters within the fort confines. Beneath the hill the Indian affairs building was erected. Sinclair's troops provided most of the labor, as would their successors for future construction projects.

After Sinclair commited himself to relocating the garrison, the local civilians weighed the advantages and disadvantages of moving to Mackinac Island. If they went, they would lose their houses. On the other hand, the island afforded them more protection from "Indian insults" and enemy attacks. It would also be easier to get provisions brought in by water, since a good harbor existed. The dense woods offered a readily accessible supply of firewood, and the soil appeared to be more fertile. Futhermore, they could conveniently take fish from the lake to supplement their diet. Since the government was deeply involved in regulating affairs between the Indians and traders, it was important that the traders locate themselves near the government's outpost. Thus, the civilians had little choice but to move and at their own expense.

Both civilians and the military transported their possessions by water or over the ice in winter. The sloops *Felicity, Welcome,* and *Hope* not only brought people and property from the mainland to the island, but delivered provisions and men from Detroit to Mackinac. Sinclair's men dismantled some of the buildings within the old fort and pulled them across the ice. Among these structures were the barracks, King's storehouse, and guardhouse.

The Church of Ste. Anne was also moved during the winter of 1780-81 along with the priest's house. It was not reconstructed inside the fort as it had been, but instead was placed in the trader's village. This act keenly illustrated Sinclair's understanding that, since many of the traders were French Canadians and practicing Roman Catholics, the removal of the church would draw them to the island and ensure their right to religious freedom.

The FELICITY *recently painted by Homer Lynn. Courtesy – Mr. Homer Lynn, Saukville, Wisconsin.*

Having completed considerable work on the new outpost, Sinclair finally got a deed for Mackinac Island from the local Chippewa Indians on May 12, 1781. The Indians had left the year before, after Sinclair persuaded them that Britain would put the island to good use. He explained that the upper ground would be fortified, with no Indians allowed in it. He also conveyed his intention "to make corn fields of the whole Island." The Indian agent's house was to be located in the village. Chief Kitchi Negon or Grand Sable, Pouanas Kousse, and Magousseihigan surrendered all Chippewa claims to the Island of Michilimackinac to the British King, George III, in exchange for five thousand pounds New York currency. Several local traders witnessed the transaction that legally gave their government control of this strategic island.

An adept politician, Sinclair proposed to name the new fort in honor of his commander. Haldimand withstood this attempt to flatter his ego and insisted that the island continue to be called Michilimackinac and the fort "be styled Fort Makinac." He maintained that it was unwise to change names of places that had been commonly used by the people for a long time. However, the bay which became the island's harbor still bears his name. For many years after, Michilimackinac and Mackinac were used interchangeably to mean the island, the fort, or both.

5

More than lumber and stone were necessary to construct Fort Mackinac. Horses and oxen aided the soldiers in moving heavy building materials. However, Mackinac Island was in short supply of these creatures. On numerous occasions, Sinclair pleaded in vain for more working animals. Yet, the presence of the few cattle meant that hay had to be acquired and men were dispatched to the mainland to gather an adequate supply.

As the artisans, soldiers, and traders moved their possessions and built new dwellings, the Indian trade prospered. For many years the military was involved directly or indirectly in Indian affairs, with the British officers most deeply engaged. During the 1780's several thousand Chippewas and Ottawas resorted to Mackinac to trade. In addition, traders transacted business with Indians further west.

In order to ensure the friendship of the Indians the government annually gave them numerous presents. The huge cost of Indian gifts caused great consternation to the Mackinac commander's superiors in Quebec. Annual expenses for Indian goods ran as high as fifty thousand pounds a year. When Sinclair submitted drafts for these large sums, his superiors were appalled. Both he and his successor, Captain Daniel Robertson, were constantly urged to reduce the number of presents given out. Yet, an invoice sent to Sinclair in May of 1782 indicates that he received over six hundred pair of blankets, eighty-two dozen linen ruffled shirts, 137 pounds of vermillion, ninety-eight dozen butcher knives, 1,080 one-pound rolls of tobacco, 4,500 flints, 2,100 pounds of gunpowder, and thousands of other objects.

An American officer checking a fur trader's license.

6

It was very difficult for Sinclair and Robertson to keep down costs. Many times expected goods arrived weeks after they were needed. As a result, it was necessary to purchase articles from private sources at a higher price. In an effort to achieve economy, they sometimes bought directly from the Indians. In 1782 Robertson purchased the entire supply of corn, about two thousand bags, from the Indian village at L'Arbre Croche, to prevent the traders from acquiring this commodity and selling it to the government at an inflated price.

Captain Robertson wrestled with the expense of Indian presents throughout his command. When Indians came to the island for gifts, the government also provided for their physical needs. Although they camped along the shoreline, they ate many valuable rations. To cut down the number of Indians coming, in 1783 Robertson sent a trader, George McBeath, to Prairie du Chien to dispense the presents there. Robertson estimated that this action would keep one thousand Indians away from Mackinac and hopefully save money.

If proper attention were not given the Indians, the British feared they might become angry and retaliate. Hence the dilemma of trying to economize and yet prevent hostilities faced the fort's commanders. In the summer of 1784 Robertson thought the Ottawas were restless and might attack the fort and island. As a result, he placed twenty men on guard each night. They were reinforced by a civilian guard of villagers. He believed this threat was due in part to the Ottawas' conviction that the British were welching on the presents they gave.

On some occasions the Indians, the military, and the civilians became involved in legal proceedings. In July, 1792 a Chippewa Indian tried to stab a trader and two companions. Men witnessing the incident subdued

An 1820 sketch of Mackinac Island from Henry R. Schoolcraft's ETHNOLOGICAL RE-
SEARCHES AMONG THE RED MAN *(1854).*

the assailant, bound him, and led him to the fort, wanting to hand him over to the commander for judicial action. During their walk up the hill, seven men attacked the party, savagely beating and knifing the defenseless Chippewa. Only the arrival of Captains Charlton and Doyle stopped the assault, but it was too late to save the Indian's life. The seven were confined in the guardhouse until noon the next day, at which time they were released on bail posted by local merchants. What further actions, if any, were taken against the men are not known, but both the Indians and the villagers appeared satisfied with the proceedings. Although most instances of interaction between the army and the villagers were not so sensational as this, the military was extensively involved in the community of Mackinac Island for over a century.

During the first few years of their presence at Fort Mackinac, the soldiers established the routines that were to characterize life for those who served later. They spent countless hours swinging axes, walking guard, and building fortifications. The post gardens were planted shortly after the occupation of the fort. When they were not engaged in these duties, the men drilled, maneuvered, and practiced with their muskets and cannon.

Although Mackinac was a long way from the army's headquarters, inspectors came to see first hand the condition of the installation. One of the earliest inspections was made in 1788 by Captain Gother Mann, Commander of the Royal Engineers, who made some penetrating observations after his visit to the fort. He said it was "too well designed for defense against musquetry . . . too ill-judged to withstand cannon . . . particularly at the rear." This was a reference to the unfortified elevation rising about 150 feet above the fort several hundred yards behind it. Mann felt 150 men were needed to defend Mackinac adequately. He also described the barracks as "in indifferent repair," the powder magazine, in "pretty good order," and the officers' stone quarters, "about half finished." Such visits and reports helped to bring about changes and improvements at the fort.

It did not take very long for the British garrison to construct quarters and rudimentary fortifications on Mackinac Island. The soldiers worked hard and spent many long and lonely evenings at this island fortress. Their experience started a life style that hundreds of men would follow during the next century. Soldiers at Mackinac were to be confronted with drill, fatigue, gardening, guard duties and a host of other responsibilities. However, not all would be work, as these men found ways to entertain themselves when they were off duty. Yet, when the bugle sounded or the drummer beat reveille at 5 a.m., the men arose and went to work.

II.

DRILL, GUARD,...

The men at Mackinac devoted much time to military exercises and activities. They policed the fort, guarded it against intruders and fire, and conducted maneuvers to improve their military skills. The officers drilled their troops and required target practice for them. To make sure that the men gave proper care to their uniforms and weapons, the post command held frequent inspections. Every year or two the post had to prepare itself for inspectors sent out by the army to evaluate the state of affairs at the fort.

Of all its responsibilities, the garrison gave top priority to ensuring the security of the fort. Each morning the guard was mounted and was not relieved until the following day. After the Americans first took command of Mackinac in 1796, Major Henry Burbeck issued orders that the guard was to consist of nine privates and a non-commissioned officer. He also requested that each man be clean and in uniform. Only when it rained or snowed were the guards allowed to remain inside. Each sentry carried his musket when he walked his post, and he could not allow admittance to the fort to any civilian without the approval of the officer of the day. For a time, an interesting maneuver marked the end of a soldier's guard duty. Under an officer's supervision, he went behind the fort and fired his musket hoping to hit a target. The individual who made the best shot each day received a gill of whiskey.

Sentinels not only watched for civilians who attempted to enter the fort, they also regulated the exits and entrances of soldiers. The commandant instructed them to allow no enlisted man to depart from the fort without leave. They kept a look-out for any thirsty man who might

9

try to sneak to the village for an evening of wine and song. At times the men on watch checked each man that left for the village, looking for extra rations or clothes that might be exchanged for liquor. The guard served as a control point for the passage of people in and out of the fort.

The guardhouse served as the headquarters for the sentries. Not only were prisoners kept here, but there were bunks for the guards, not walking post, to sleep until their turn to watch arrived. In addition, the non-commissioned officer in charge had a desk from which he conducted his business. He saw to it that no whiskey, other than the ration, was drunk by the men on duty. He also made sure that all the fires in the barracks had been put out after taps and that the storehouse door was locked. Other responsibilities of the corporal included making sure that the sentinels were relieved every two hours, that all lights were out after taps, and that his men remained awake. Between taps and reveille the sentry in the fort proclaimed "All is well" every fifteen minutes; the one at the Commanding Officer's quarters answered him to acknowledge that everything was under control.

Every man feared fire. This posed a far greater threat to the community than the possibility of Indian attacks or intruders. If the sentinel spotted a fire, either in the fort or in the village, he was to yell "Fire!" and to alert the corporal of the guard and the commanding officer. After informing the village residents, he returned to the fire and assisted in the efforts to stop the blaze. Villagers and soldiers worked together to put

A lonely sentry standing guard above south sally port. Courtesy – Clarke Library, Central Michigan University.

10

down any fires in the fort, as well as in town. A devastating fire could wipe out the entire island community if it got out of hand and was fanned by a strong breeze. Consequently, the guard exercised great care to make sure that the water buckets were filled and that all fires in the buildings were put out.

Despite these precautions, the men fought a number of serious fires throughout the years. The British witnessed the old guardhouse burn in 1783. Lieutenant Colonel William Lawrence strongly commended his troops for putting out a blaze on the roof of a blockhouse in 1819. The men who took part in this effort displayed exemplary courage since a quantity of gunpowder was stored on the floor directly beneath the rafters. Occasionally the guard spotted flames in new buildings. In 1827 the post hospital burned just before its completion; thirty-one years later the men saw their brand new barracks go up in smoke. Only three years earlier the old barracks had been destroyed by fire. Not only did the soldiers lose their living quarters, but many personal belongings as well. Until new accommodations could be constructed, the men lived wherever there was room, usually in the blockhouses. Given the personal hardships and losses created by fire, it was not surprising that the garrison took its fire watch and fire fighting responsibilities quite seriously.

Due to the fact that the men spent so much time working, the amount of time allowed for drill was limited. In addition, the severe cold made outdoor exercises impractical during the winter. Despite these difficulties, the men mastered the basic exercises. In 1819 the garrison devoted two hours a day, six days a week to drill. Captain Benjamin K. Pierce insisted that these maneuvers be "very exact" and that the men be in full uniform. This impressed the importance of strict discipline and precision upon the new recruits. His efforts shaped his troops into a respectable unit and drew commendation from Major General Jacob Brown when he inspected Pierce's men late in the summer. Brown praised the officers and the men, saying "The precision and accuracy in the infantry maneuvers and artillery exercises evidenced a knowledge of military duty highly honorable to the division."

Not all inspection reports were as flattering. Several years later Major General Edmund Pendleton Gaines found that the troops could handle axes and brooms better than muskets, in addition to being imprecise in their exercise of military movements. Despite these shortcomings, Gaines recognized the hardships endured by the garrison, and he believed their knowledge of manual exercises and marching was as good as the circumstances allowed. Survival in the cold required that chopping wood take precedence over drill.

Perhaps no unit while at the fort drilled more rigorously than Company L of the Fourth Artillery. Captain Thomas Williams laid out a very intensive schedule in September, 1854 for his troops. Five mornings a week the recruits formed themselves on the parade ground at 5:00 a.m. for instruction. They also drilled for two more hours each day. During the course of the week, this unit practiced infantry parade and bayonet exercises three times and underwent instruction in the use of artillery twice. Along with these exercises went target practice with both muskets and cannon.

The divisional inspections occurred at the most once a year. However, the officers inspected their troops every week on Sunday mornings. Each man made sure his weapon was clean and in working order. Uniforms were to be clean and neat. If these requirements were not satisfied, a recruit or veteran could expect a good chewing out by his company commander. The commandant watched the men go through their exercises, pointing out any sloppy or inaccurate movements. He also complimented the men for good performances. The officers instructed their men to take pride in their work, as the competency of an officer's troops reflected on his own abilities. A well-disciplined company brought recognition to the officers and non-commissioned officers of that unit.

While the men were required to perform on the drill field, the cadre received instructions on the art of war. In the late 1860's both the officers and the non-com's attended two classes a week studying new regulations and tactics. They gained knowledge from Upton's *Infantry Tactics, Bayonet Exercise, Articles of War,* and *The Revised Army Regulations.* Much of what they learned, they drilled into their men on the parade ground.

Soldiers relaxing on parade ground. Note the little boy standing next to the corporal on the left.

Although the soldiers usually spent only an hour or two a day on the drill field, they put in very long days. The musicians sounded their bugle or drum and fife throughout the day to signal the time. In July, 1874, Captain Charles J. Dickey posted the following list of signals:

Reveille	5:00 A.M.
Breakfast call	5:30
Surgeon's call	6:30
Fatigue call	7:00
Guard mounting 1st call	7:50
2nd call	8:00
Drill call	10:00
Recall from drill	11:00
Recall from fatigue	11:30
Orderly call	11:45
Dinner call	12:00
Fatigue call	1:00 P.M.
Drill call	2:00
Recall from drill	3:00
Recall from fatigue	one hour before sunset
Dress parade	20 minutes before sunset
Tattoo	9:00
Taps	9:30

Sundays

Inspection 1st call	7:50
2nd call	8:00
Guard mounting immediately after inspection	
Church call	10:30

Due to shorter days, the army decreased the number of work hours in winter. Breakfast call usually fell at 7:00 or 7:30, and the evening assembly at 4:00 or 4:30.

Regardless of the season, the fort had to be kept clean. Consequently, a small contingent of troops drew police duty each day. The officer of the day directed this crew to pick up any garbage or rubbish that was lying about and remove it. It was their responsibility to sweep out the barracks and to see to it that the men aired their blankets. When the rooms were dirty, the police washed them. They also cared for the roads leading to and behind the fort, picking up rubble and animal dung as well as repairing minor damage. After finishing these jobs, they performed such minor maintenance tasks as replacing broken windows, fixing loose steps, and putting new shingles on building roofs when needed. In the winter Mother Nature gave them other chores, shoveling snow or thawing out frozen water pipes.

Company musicians in formation.

In addition to paying close attention to the physical condition of the fort, the men spent much time caring for military hardware. Not only did they have to keep their muskets or rifles in firing condition, but they had to load or make cartridges for their weapons. It was not uncommon for their muskets to be old and not in good firing order. The inspector general complained several times about the antiquated arms being used by the garrison. The several cannon employed had to be kept in working order. This proved to be quite difficult, as the elements eroded the wooden carriages. Frequently, the inspection reports pointed out their delapidated condition. The men also prepared the charges used to fire the cannon either for practice or to commemorate an important event or the arrival of an important person. Cleaning the muskets, rifles and cannon was a dirty but necessary function.

Despite the fact that the soldiers did not have to use their arms in military engagements at Fort Mackinac after 1815, they fired them often, particularly after the Springfield 45-70 rifle became the standard weapon issued to the men. After the Civil War, the troops spent many hours on the rifle ranges. The six-hundred-yard range was located behind the fort with the men firing into the hill beneath Fort Holmes. It had two revolving targets at which the sharpshooters aimed. In the mid-1880's, the troops built a one-thousand-yard range in the island's interior. On this site, Willard telephones were used to relay the results of a shooter's attempt to hit the target and to give the next man the all-clear to commence firing.

Due to winter's snow and cold the men usually shot only between May and November. This created some problems for the post command. As the number of summer residents and visitors increased, particularly after the National Park was created in 1875, their comfort and safety had to be considered. It was essential that no person using the park got in the way of a bullet fired at a target on the range. The marksmen exercised extreme caution in order not to scare any horses being ridden by a civilian or pulling a carriage. At times the smoke and the noise proved a nuisance to those in the park. A further hazard was that large clouds of smoke generated by the shooters might be mistaken for a forest fire during the dry season. Even worse was the possibility that smoke from a fire might be mistaken as the result of target practice and disregarded. Because of these dangers, the commandant limited the use of the rifle ranges to May, June, September, and October during some years.

Not all units stationed at Mackinac were infantry. In the 1850's Company L of the Fourth Artillery made the fort their home, and they brought their cannon with them. In 1853 they constructed a floating target of wood and canvas and used it in the Straits beyond Haldimand Bay. In order to provide a moving target, a boat towed the float on windy days. To the men's great displeasure, hitting the target was not their most difficult task. Each day they had to bring a cannon down the hill to the beach for practice. At day's end, using bricoles, the troops dragged the

Either the Tenth or Twenty-third Infantry in full dress for inspection in the 1880's.

15

heavy cannon up the hill to be kept in the fort. This state of affairs made Captain Williams very unhappy. Believing it quite unreasonable that there was no place to store artillery pieces or gunpowder at the bottom of the hill, he proposed converting the Indian Agency, which was used by a blacksmith, into such an arsenal. Security problems rendered his proposal unworkable.

Except during the War of 1812, the soldiers at Mackinac did not engage in combat on the island. However, their activities were affected by military events in other places. Black Hawk's uprising put the garrison in a very business-like mood in July, 1832. They did not celebrate Independence Day; they did not even fire a cannon. The commander expected his men might be ordered to Chicago to assist in the campaign against Black Hawk. Several boats loaded with troops passed through Mackinac on their way to Illinois, thereby helping to create an uneasy feeling among some of the village residents. Their fears proved unnecessary since any threat to the island was quite remote, and the army put down the uprising by late summer. In the early 1840's tensions arose between the United States and Great Britain along the Canadian border. This prompted the post command to draw up plans to refortify Fort Holmes. A major confrontation was averted when the Webster-Ashburton Treaty was agreed upon in 1842. Another scare came in 1878 when Major General Winfield Hancock alerted the post to be ready for action in Wisconsin. Indian unrest there stirred up fears that might require the help of Major Alfred L. Hough's men.

Shortly after the Civil War broke out, the regular army troops vacated Fort Mackinac. Only Ordnance Sergeant William Marshall remained behind. Although the post was used by the Stanton guards during the summer of 1862, not until August, 1867 did a regular unit return.

This abandonment of the fort came over thirty years too late to please Colonel George Croghan. In his inspection report of 1828 he recommended that the post be abandoned. He expressed the belief that it would take two thousand men to defend the island. Several years earlier General Gaines also questioned the wisdom of fortifying such an indefensible place. Certainly these men saw some of the same weaknesses as had Gother Mann in 1788. Despite these discouraging observations, the army continued to keep the post active. After 1815 the danger of an armed invasion or attack on the island was slight; hence, the supposed inability of the troops to defend the island had very little practical significance.

In the 1880's and 1890's, Mackinac Island witnessed some very extensive military operations involving five hundred or more men. Units of the National Guard and the army used the island for their summer encampments. The Michigan Militia assembled its four regiments in the park for most of July, 1888. At the same time, from Fort Wayne came Companies G and I and the band of the Twenty-third Infantry who joined Companies E and K stationed at the fort, for maneuvers. On July 11 a seventeen-gun salute from Fort Mackinac greeted the arrival of Governor Cyrus G. Luce. During the next few days he reviewed the activities of the troops. In some of the following years the Michigan Militia returned to the island for their summer activities. Units of the Ohio National Guard also encamped on the island for "health, rest, and cool air." These units usually pitched their tents and established their headquarters on the Early farm in the island's interior. On occasion they set up housekeeping in the post pastures. They came to Mackinac because of its favorable summer climate, rifle ranges, and the assistance given to them by the post command.

Not all of the garrison's summer activities took place at their home base. In 1889 they gathered at Goguac Lake with other companies of the Twenty-third Infantry and the state militia. The men worked at both manual of arms and movements. The expertise of the regulars assisted the citizen soldiers to improve their military skills. When the men returned after their ten-day stint, Richard Hulbert, a local merchant, said that they appeared "as though they had been on a Hot Indian Trail for a month, sunburned and weary." Experiences such as this helped improve the military know-how of all who participated.

Drill, guard duty, post police, maneuvers, and inspections composed a very real part of a soldier's life. He may have found these activities boring and arduous, but they had to be done. The officers and non-coms gave the orders, and the privates carried them out. Not only did a musket have to be in firing order, it had to be clean enough to satisfy his commander during inspection. Likewise, the officer of the day made sure the guard and the police did their job right; otherwise, the men might face a court-martial for disobedience of orders. A man's physical and mental well-being depended to a great extent on how well he performed his soldierly duties. For example, the recruit who could not master the manual of arms might be subjected to a considerable amount of ridicule by his superiors and his fellow soldiers. This could make his life miserable. Fortunately, the soldier involved himself in other activities, but not always by his own choice. Some were enjoyable; others, particularly fatigue, were not.

III.

FATIGUE AND EXTRA DUTY

The enlisted men spent countless hours on fatigue assignments and many frequently found themselves on extra duty. These details often involved hard physical labor and exposure to the harsh winter climate. When timber had to be cut, roads built, or the walls of the fort repaired, the soldiers usually got the job. They also performed the labor needed to keep the garrison supplied in food, fuel, and water. These tasks appeared to be endless and thankless, yet they were necessary to sustain the post.

Like the British before them, the Americans soon learned that constructing and maintaining a garrison on Mackinac Island was a prodigious task. Upon their arrival in 1796, they discovered the fort was in great disrepair. Most of the buildings were outside the walls, except for a barracks, provisions storehouse, guardhouse, powder magazine, and the officers' stone quarters. Major Henry Burbeck put his men to work strengthening the fort walls and repairing existing structures. They also extended the north wall of the fort and built three blockhouses by 1800. These were the first of a number of building projects to be undertaken by American soldiers at Mackinac.

Construction in the late eighteenth and early nineteenth centuries involved much more than simply putting up a building. With the exception of metal articles such as nails and hinges and glass, the basic materials were taken from the surrounding land. Men had to fell trees, cut timbers, saw planks and boards, and make shingles for each project. They also gathered stones, quarried limestone and kilned lime that they used. The men did much of this work in the winter, thus enduring icy winds and driving snow. Many a man cursed nature as he battled her harsh blows. Despite these hardships, the soldiers at Mackinac relentlessly pursued these operations. Not all was done in winter; during the summer of 1819 a detail of men raised a storehouse and replaced a segment of the fort walls.

A few years later, a large scale construction plan was launched. This renovation resulted in part from Colonel George Croghan's critical evaluation of the fort in 1826. Although he felt that the post should be abandoned, he believed continued occupation meant that the War Department had to institute plans "for the immediate erection of a proper work." The existing work had deteriorated to the point where it was no longer safe. For the next two years, the garrison was very busy. Some men repaired chimneys and fireplaces, others put new roofs on existing buildings, while still others prepared materials needed for all the construction activities. When the project was finished, a number of new structures had been erected, including a hospital, guardhouse, gunshed, blacksmith shop, carpenter shop, bakehouse, and a store for the Ordnance and Quartermaster Department. In addition, the old buildings were all made more comfortable and safe. On his next visit in 1828 Croghan found that the fort was in good condition.

Although the last extensive building program did not occur until the

Civilians hauling wood from Bois Blanc Island over the ice.

1870's and 1880's, several important structures were erected earlier. In 1835 the commanding officer's quarters were started. The garrison put up a new two-story barracks in 1855 and rebuilt it three years later after a fire. In 1859, the army moved the hospital to its new quarters located just east of the fort.

After Congress designated most of the military reserve on the island as a National Park, the fort became a two-company garrison. This, coupled with advances in technology and a desire by the army to make its posts more livable, prompted a major expansion of the fort's physical facilities. The soldiers kept busy erecting two houses for officers, laundress' quarters, sergeants' quarters, a bakehouse, a commissary storehouse, a reading room, and a bathhouse, plus numerous additions and improvements in existing structures. By 1885, all the buildings inside the fort were completed.

The post artisans also built boats. By 1819 they had constructed several vessels that enabled the quartermaster to move firewood, timbers, hay, and numerous other supplies needed by the garrison. He estimated that his men could build five-hundred dollar boats for sixty dollars, and that a considerable amount of money could be saved on freight charges.

Construction, though a continuing process, went ahead in spurts, but the post's need for fuel was always evident. Many details busied themselves cutting firewood. Just as important were the teams of horses to pull the wood out of the forest. Shortly after their arrival at Mackinac, the American soldiers began supplying the post with fuel. Major Burbeck ordered the post adjutant to make two teams available to bring one and one-half cords of wood into the fort each day. He put Sergeant Loomis in charge of an eight-man party with each soldier expected to cut and pile one cord a day.

After the island's supply had been exhausted early in the nineteenth century, men were dispatched to Bois Blanc Island, several miles from Mackinac, to harvest trees on government land. Usually details spent many days at a time on Bois Blanc, cutting trees and stacking firewood. During the winter of 1834-35, the troops cut over six hundred cords of wood that the horses hauled through two feet of snow to a clearing near the shoreline. From here much of it was transported twelve miles to Mackinac over the ice.

To move a team and sled over the ice, a competent teamster was required. This could be a very hazardous business. One had to look out for cracks in the ice and make sure that he did not get off the marked track. A sudden change in the weather could bring a blinding snow to obscure a man's vision and result in his getting lost. Despite one's skills and precautions, accidents still happened. In March of 1849 the quartermaster sent a public team to Cheboygan to get a load of boards from the sawmill. Upon learning of a thin spot of ice along the route to Cheboygan, Lieutenant William Beall located the place and waited, wanting to warn the teamster on his return. Unknown to Beall, the driver's sled broke down, causing a delay while a replacement was procured. When he finally got going, he met Beall along the way and bypassed the hazard without incident. However, on his return to Cheboygan a sudden snowstorm caused him to get off the path, onto the thin ice. The horses fell through and drowned in the cold water. Fortunately, the man escaped without any serious injury.

By the middle of the 1800's, the army found it more efficient to purchase its firewood by contract. This also helped to raise the morale of the men, who no longer had to endure the winter hardships on Bois Blanc. A private contractor from the village cut the trees on government lands and delivered the finished product to the post woodyard. Various bids reveal the cost at between three and four dollars per cord. In 1850 Edward A. Franks received the contract to furnish 330 cords at $3.48 per cord.

The great demand for wood made tools quite valuable. In 1798 each company received three axes and two iron wedges for which the company commanders were responsible. If an ax head needed repair, the company paid for it by having a pint of whiskey withheld from its rations. When one man could be held responsible, he assumed the cost of the

These men of Company F, First Infantry, relax while on fatigue in 1870. Courtesy – Clarke Library, Central Michigan University.

damage. To insure that the men took proper care of these implements, they had to produce them each week at inspection. Whenever a noncommissioned officer took parties into the woods to cut trees, he was held accountable for any lost equipment. This great concern for iron tools was necessary because of the scarcity of these articles.

The troops put their tools to work in 1843, converting the ground behind the fort into a respectable drill field. Although most of the trees had already been removed, the land was uneven and rocky. They levelled the three- or four-acre plot and spread gravel over it. After this was finished, the men built a fence. As a result, a large and safe area was created for military drills. Undoubtedly, some of the soldiers found the fruits of their labor to be quite bitter.

Just as vital as wood, water was essential to the post's existence. Although surrounded by great bodies of water, getting adequate supplies up the hill always presented serious problems. Throughout the fort's history various wells and springs provided some of the precious liquid, but when these sources failed, lake water was used. In the fort's southeast corner the British dug a well which proved to be quite unreliable. In later years the Americans dug one behind the fort which did not solve the water problem either. In the 1880's water was pumped up the hill from a spring beneath the bluff to a reservoir located in the north blockhouse. Initially a one-inch lead pipe carried water to the mess rooms in the barracks. Later the army extended the pipe system to other buildings in the fort. The wooden tank held sixty-five barrels, which was a three-day supply in summer and five in winter. To prevent the pipes from freezing, the builders installed a valve at the lowest point of each one where the water could be drained.

When these facilities did not operate, many soldiers and horses labored strenuously hauling water up the hill in tanks filled at the lakefront. The garrison used many gallons for drinking, cooking, washing, laundering, and putting out fires. The men discovered one way to get water was to collect it during rainy days. To accomplish this, they put gutters on building roofs to catch the run-off and to funnel it into barrels and cisterns that had been built to hold water for fire fighting purposes. Great efforts were made to keep an adequate supply on hand in case of fire. The post police filled a number of buckets at the guardhouse and the hospital each day. In 1853 eight cisterns were built in the cellars of some buildings. Unfortunately these proved to be very impractical. When the barracks caught on fire in 1855, the smoke was so thick in the basement that the fire fighters could not reach the one located there.

Another chore created by the threat of fire was the construction of ladders on the roof of each building. With these, several fire fighters could mount the roof and receive buckets of water from those on the ground. In this way a blaze on a rooftop could be doused if it was discovered before it got out of control.

In an effort to improve the fort's sanitation facilities, the army installed a modern tile drainage system in 1889. This allowed all of the sewage to flow into the lake. Artisans put in plumbing to care for wastes and water from the enlisted men's quarters and the bathhouse. The work that the troops performed while building the structure and putting in the plumbing was richly rewarded, as they found it much easier to keep clean in the bathhouse's six new tubs.. In addition, the kitchen sinks drained into the system. This convenience added greatly to the men's comfort.

The commandant frequently assigned men to work under the quartermaster's direction. Since the quartermaster was responsible for transporting all of the supplies and goods used at the garrison, he needed a lot of assistance. One of his never-ending problems was securing feed for the animals. Before the 1830's he sent out details of eight or ten men to cut hay on the mainland. Once cut, it had to be hauled ten to fifteen miles over both land and water. Obviously, this was a very expensive and time consuming job. To save both time and money hay was purchased from a contractor by the mid-1830's. In 1835 alone over eighteen tons of timothy and clover were needed. Lieutenant James Penrose agreed to buy the hay from Michael Dousman for twenty-eight dollars a ton; however, a dispute arose between the two and Penrose bought it from another merchant. In later years Dousman did supply the post stables with hay.

A winter fatigue party confronted with large quantities of snow. Courtesy – Mackinac Island Historical Society.

Not only was the procurement of hay a problem, getting enough draft animals at times posed a more serious difficulty. Due to the fort's location on a hill on an island, the power of oxen or horses was absolutely necessary to maintain the garrison. When a horse died or got too old to work, it had to be quickly replaced or the troops would be in trouble. The quartermaster disposed of two worn-out horses in 1821 and urgently requested permission to buy a new team. If this were not done, he would have been unable to furnish an ample supply of wood for the winter.

The presence of horses, pigs, cows, and chickens meant that someone had to care for them. A soldier or two spent some of his fatigue duty feeding the animals and milking the cows. He also had the unpleasant task of cleaning the manure out of the stable. Much of this was spread on the nearby post gardens.

Many vegetables grew in the gardens and the men performed the necessary labor. In 1820 Captain Benjamin K. Pierce ordered each company commander to select one private to serve as company gardener. When help was needed, additional men went down the hill to hoe weeds or till the soil in preparation for planting. It took a lot of work to keep several acres productive, yet it was definitely worth it, as this was the fort's only source of fresh vegetables. They harvested some good sized yields; in 1890 the gardeners produced 1,150 bushels of potatoes and over two thousand heads of cabbage.

The quartermaster kept fatigues busy doing a variety of others jobs. Whenever a boat arrived with supplies or equipment for the garrison, he sent men to the docks to bring the goods to the fort. They loaded the cargo on wagons and delivered it to its proper destination. They replenished the commissary's provisions, brought the ordnance supplies to the storage areas, and moved new stoves and any other equipment acquired by the garrison. In addition, they installed any new apparatus such as water pumps, stoves, and sinks. While these activities were going on, others carried wood into the fort and conveyed the day's rations to the kitchens.

Winter snows also kept fatigues busy. The men had to shovel pathways inside the fort as well as keep the north sally port open. When snow piled high upon the roofs, they cleared the roofs to eliminate the danger of collapse. Outside, they removed snow from the stairs leading to the south sally port and made sure the stables could be reached. Whenever ice formed in dangerous places, the fatigue details had to remove it.

Since most of Mackinac Island was under the control of the War Department, the garrison built and maintained any roads the army deemed necessary. Details cleared away trees and brush that blocked the path of new roadways. When necessary, the men graded the terrain and brought in fill that might be needed. After the national park was created, the roads received considerably more use. Hence, the maintenance problems increased. Fatigues or men on special duty were sent out to erect new fences and to repair those that were damaged. They kept up roads along both the east and west bluffs so that summer cottagers had access to their properties. In addition, they removed trees that might have fallen across a road and any debris that would impede travel and detract from the island's beauty.

There was a significant difference between fatigue and extra duty. Fatigue involved various kinds of work assignments that were less than ten days long. Projects undertaken by details on fatigue might take an hour or week to perform, but they were considered part of a soldier's regular duty. When a man was put on extra duty, he received extra pay for his labors. Army regulations emphasized that these assignments had to be of at least ten days duration. Men placed on extra duty were usually involved in major projects such as building fortifications, cutting timbers, or performing large tasks away from the garrison. While on extra duty, men generally devoted all their time to the required labor and did not drill. Fatigue details often took up only a portion of a soldier's day.

Extra duty assignments usually involved hard work and caused some dissatisfaction among the men. Spending several weeks in February on

Viewing tower at Fort Holmes built by soldiers in 1886.

25

Bois Blanc Island did not appeal to most soldiers; neither did a trip to the mainland to gather hay. Despite these hardships, extra duty gave a man a chance to supplement his monthly pay. The *Army Regulations* for 1812 authorized an additional wage of ten cents a day and one gill of spirits; by 1881 privates and non-commissioned officers received twenty-five cents per day. Men employed as artificers or skilled workers got forty cents a day. Although most of the troops disliked going on extra duty, they found that the additional money came in handy at the sutler's store or the village saloons.

The number of men serving on extra duty varied greatly from time to time as it depended on the garrison's labor needs. During periods of extensive building, quite a few soldiers were employed as artisans. In September, 1876, thirteen men were employed in new construction. Four men served as carpenters, three as teamsters, three as laborers, and one each as a painter, a blacksmith, and a mason. On some occasions the post command hired civilian craftsmen to assist the troops in construction projects. This was done where the garrison had insufficient skills or manpower to complete a project.

The army relied upon the labors of its soldiers because it seemed to be the most economical way of getting things done. Sixty or seventy men provided a handy source of labor. Since the government was already feeding, clothing, and housing these men, it was quite logical that they be employed in military construction projects. Yet the army learned that it was to its advantage to contract for wood and animal feed. The cost of paying men extra pay and transporting men and supplies became too high. In addition, the effect that these projects had upon morale created more problems. Unhappy soldiers tended to desert or get into trouble, which proved quite expensive in time and money.

However, the commandant continued to use soldiers for construction jobs on the island. These duties created less hardships for the men as they did not have to leave the comforts of the post. The officers also found it easier to supervise projects close to home. Despite this, many men still found these extra duties to be against their concept of what ought to be a soldier's duties. They realized little fulfillment in cutting trees, grading roads, hauling lumber, or building fences. Much of this work was tiring, boring, and very difficult.

The net result of fatigue and extra duty was that the army got its work done. Normally, the government did not consider the enlisted man's wishes when undertaking large scale building programs. If fortifications were to be constructed, the soldiers would do it. After all, that was one of the reasons the government hired them. Likewise the maintenance work required to keep a garrison running had to be performed by the troops. Since the soldiers at Fort Mackinac rarely got involved in military engagements, they had to be kept busy in order to keep them out of mischief. After 1815 the British were gone and no Indians attacked the post. If the post command had not put the men to work, it was quite likely that idleness would have been more burdensome than the unpleasant extra duties and fatigues. The soldiers' monotonous labor did have some healthy effects, even though most of the men would have disagreed. In addition, physical work and drill were more favorable activities than combat.

Soldiers on fatigue inside north sally port. Courtesy – Clarke Library, Central Michigan University.

IV.

WAR

To their good fortune, fate spared most of the soldiers at Fort Mackinac from the pangs of battle. Yet, British and American troops found themselves locked in combat on several occasions between 1812 and 1814. These battles tested the courage of the men and the military ability of their officers. Planning and poor communication played important roles in the outcome of the skirmishes fought over control of Fort Mackinac.

The garrison was often directly affected by events that occurred hundreds and thousands of miles away. In the early nineteenth century, war between Great Britain and France resulted in the interruption of American commercial activities on the Atlantic Ocean. The United States' efforts to avoid direct involvement in this conflict proved futile, and in 1812 the United States and Great Britain went to war. This meant action for the Redcoats garrisoned at St. Joseph's Island and the Yankees on Mackinac Island.

Although the war broke out on June 18, the American commander, Lieutenant Porter Hanks, did not learn of it until July 17. Poor communication kept Hanks and his men ignorant of this new situation. His sixty-one men had been trained to fight, but when the time came to defend the post, all of their preparations were in vain. While the sentries walked their post during the early morning hours of July 17, a British force commanded by Captain Charles Roberts landed at the rear of the island. He had learned of the war's declaration a couple of weeks earlier from Toussaint Pothier, a fur trader, who had come to St. Joseph to protect his company's trade goods located there. By July 8, the efficient British General Isaac Brock had officially informed Roberts that a state of war existed.

British and Indian forces await the American landing on August 4, 1814.

Roberts' force consisted of forty-seven regulars, 150 voyageurs, and several hundred Indians. The practice of using Indian warriors was consistent with previous seventeenth-and eighteenth-century North American wars. By using native allies, the British were able to increase their forces and deprive their enemy of Indian assistance. The British convinced their Indian warriors it was to their advantage that the English be victorious. If the Americans won, they would not be friendly to the Indians and would deprive them of the presents and goods the British had been supplying. The Canadian voyageurs who joined in this venture also had an interest to protect. With Britain in control of the upper Great Lakes, the fur trade would be more lucrative for British subjects. All of these auxiliaries did much to strengthen this unit of the Tenth Royal Veteran Battalion, composed of older men who had previously been discharged after their tour of duty had expired.

The British came from St. Joseph's Island aboard the schooner *Caledonia* and several batteaux. They spent a sleepless night en route to Mackinac, hoping to overtake the unsuspecting American garrison. As they approached Mackinac Island, the British intercepted and captured Michael Dousman. He had been sent to St. Joseph by Lieutenant Hanks to spy on British activity. From Dousman, Roberts discovered that the Americans were unaware war had been declared.

Learning this, Roberts released Dousman with the understanding he would not inform Hanks of British intentions. Rather, Dousman was to warn the villagers to take refuge. Roberts hoped to capture Fort Mackinac with a minimum of bloodshed by surprising Hanks. The British captain had no desire to see any civilians needlessly killed.

His Majesty's forces not only had the element of surprise on their side, but also the advantage of superior numbers. The bulk of these men were Indian auxiliaries. Through the efforts of the fur trader Robert Dickson, over one hundred Sioux, Menominee, and Winnebago braves joined the war party. In addition John Askin, Jr. persuaded nearly three hundred Ottawa and Chippewa to join in this venture. The presence of these men added greatly to the attackers firepower, but also created headaches for Roberts. These warriors did not observe the same discipline as did the British regulars and the Canadians. Hence, Roberts feared he would be unable to control the Indians once the battle began. The result could have been catastrophic for the island's inhabitants.

This fear was the result of differing concepts of war. The British and American armies fought under certain rules or understandings that allowed humane treatment for many participants and victims of war. Prisoners were not shot or imprisoned but were paroled to their own country, thereby sparing them much hardship. If civilians were willing

A cap plate from an artillerist, about 1815, found at Fort Mackinac.

30

to follow orders, generally they were not harmed and were allowed to keep their personal property. The Indians, however, viewed war as a means of destroying their enemy. Consequently they had less respect for property and civilian lives than their British allies.

During the early morning darkness, Roberts and his troops landed on the island's northwest shore. He realized that the hill behind the garrison commanded the fort and that a cannon placed there would render the Americans defenseless. Some of Roberts' Canadians lugged one of the six-pounders to the top of the hill. When he was warned early in the morning of the British presence, Lieutenant Hanks realized there was little he could do to prevent the capture of the post. American soldiers could see British soldiers and Indians on the heights behind the fort. Understanding the gravity of the situation, Hanks awaited Roberts' next move.

Suspense and uncertainty gripped the Americans at the presence of this hostile force. Battle would mean death and injury to some of the men. Their fears increased when the British fired their cannon, formally making known their presence. Roberts then sent down a demand that the post be surrendered "to His Britannic Majesty's forces." Three islanders who were taken prisoners came with the truce flag to plead for the acceptance of Roberts' terms. Ambrose Davenport, Samuel Abbott, and John Dousman informed Hanks that the British had a large force and were well equipped. The only way needless bloodshed could be avoided was for Hanks to turn the fort over to Roberts without offering any resistance.

Some of the tension was relieved thirty minutes later when Hanks surrendered Fort Mackinac to the invaders. The articles of capitulation affected the entire island community. The American soldiers became prisoners of war. Some of the men must have welcomed this for they were paroled to the United States on condition they would no longer serve in the army until the war ended. This seemingly generous provision applied only to about two-thirds of Hanks troops. Three men were accused of being deserters from the British army, and another twenty were taken into the King's service because they were allegedly British subjects.

The civilians were given a choice of swearing allegiance to the King or leaving within thirty days. Only Michael Dousman was allowed to remain without taking an oath; most other villagers became British subjects. Making this switch was of little consequence to people whose primary concern was business. Many of these individuals were former British subjects, and they had developed little loyalty for the weak, distant United States government. Roberts guaranteed the sanctity of private property. Despite his fear that some of his Indian warriors might get out of hand and violate civilian rights, it fortunately did not happen. In addition, all merchant vessels and their cargo were to remain in the possession of their owners. This was not true of government property. All provisions, trade goods, and furs found in the fort or the government trading factory were confiscated.

The somewhat embarrassed Porter Hanks was paroled to Detroit. A court of inquiry convened on August 15 to investigate and to pass judgment on the way he performed his duties. The fact that he had surrendered his post without a fight created suspicions about his conduct. This court never rendered a decision for the unlucky Hanks was killed the next day by a cannon ball during the British attack on Detroit.

A year later ill health forced Captain Roberts, the British commandant, to resign his position, and in September, 1813 he turned over the command to Captain Richard Bullock. Some of the civilians loyal to Britain questioned Bullock's competency and ability to handle men. Despite this dissatisfaction with his leadership, distant events made the British position at Fort Mackinac quite tenuous. Captain Oliver Hazard Perry had defeated the British navy on Lake Erie on September 10, and several weeks later General William Henry Harrison whipped the British at the Battle of the Thames. The Americans next target was Fort Mackinac. Fortunately for Bullock and his men, the cold season was too near and Harrison's plans to capture Mackinac were delayed.

The British endured great hardships that winter. Unable to get adequate provisions from supply depots on Lake Erie, the soldiers faced the

The view of Fort Mackinac that Captain Charles Roberts had from Fort Holmes. This picture, taken in the late 1890's, shows the 600-yard rifle range.

possibility of starvation. This was avoided when commissary officer William Bailey purchased food supplies from people living in the surrounding area. Yet, by March the entire meat supply had been exhausted, which left the men with a diet of fish and corn.

When spring finally arrived, the British troops feared an American attack. To meet this expected assault, Bullock improved the fortifications on the island. In addition to shoring up Fort Mackinac's walls, he built a blockhouse atop the heights behind the fort, naming it Fort George. These measures protected the garrison from a land attack, but they still feared a naval barrage from the American navy. Some of the British anxieties were relieved when a number of boats loaded with supplies cruised into the harbor in May, 1814. On board was the new post commander, Lieutenant Colonel Robert McDouall.

Several weeks after his arrival McDouall received some bad news. The British trading post at Prairie du Chien had been overrun in May by the Americans led by General William Clark. This event frightened the Winnebago Indians living at Prairie du Chien as several of their men were killed by Clark's troops. In an effort to regain control of the post McDouall authorized an expedition to drive the Americans out of Wisconsin. A fur trader, William McKay, was put in charge of this force composed of Winnebago and Sioux Indians and volunteers of the militia or Michigan Fencibles. These Indians and citizen soldiers routed the American force on July 20. This good news buoyed the spirits of McDouall's men at Mackinac who were about to confront the American navy and army.

Fortunately for McDouall the Americans proved inept in their naval operations. After disputes over who was to be put in command of the army's troops, Lieutenant Colonel George Croghan finally was appointed to lead an expedition of more than seven hundred soldiers to Mackinac. Second in command was Major Andrew Hunter Holmes. The fleet assembled to transport the men and carry out the mission included the *Lawrence*, the *Niagara*, the *Scorpion*, the *Tigress*, and the *Caledonia*. This naval force, commanded by Captain Arthur Sinclair, first sailed to St. Joseph Island and burned the abandoned British fort there. While in the area, they also raided the Indian trading post at Sault Ste. Marie.

Having finished these preliminaries, Sinclair decided to make things interesting for the Redcoats on Mackinac Island. On July 26 the American fleet arrived at the Straits. When British cannon fire drove them from their anchorage near Round Island, the Americans drifted further eastward towards Bois Blanc Island. On the following day Sinclair discovered, while dueling the British, that the thirty-two pound cannon on his ships, the *Lawrence* and the *Niagara*, could not be sufficiently raised to reach the fort. Hence plans for a head-on assault had to be abandoned.

Frustrated by this effort, Croghan hoped to dislodge the British through a land campaign. Consequently, on August 4 Sinclair sailed his fleet to the site of the British landing two years earlier. From here Croghan led his force to the shore and through the trees to an open field where he hoped to dig in. However, McDouall had stationed his men on the other end of the field. His force of 140 soldiers and militia, 350 Indians and an artillery battery fired on the invaders when they appeared at the field's edge.

American artillery returned the British fire, but were off target. The British barrage created confusion among the Americans. British bullets cut down Major Andrew Hunter Holmes and Captain Dusha. The loss of these officers created disorder among the Americans. The British position was too strong and their men too well disciplined for Croghan's troops. Several hours after the battle began, it ended with an American retreat. As they left, they counted their casualties, which included thirteen killed and fifty-one wounded. Among the dead was Major Holmes.

Despite this failure, the American forces still had the capacity to choke the British if an effective blockade could be set up. Since all transportation to Fort Mackinac was by water, naval control of Lake Huron by the Americans would prevent the British from supplying their garrison. After destroying a British blockhouse on the Nottawasaga River and capturing the *Nancy*, a schooner loaded with supplies bound for Mackinac, Croghan and Sinclair took the *Niagara* back to Detroit. They left the *Scorpion* and the *Tigress* near St. Joseph's with express orders to prevent any supply boats from getting past them to Mackinac. In keeping with their previous military operations, the Americans found this task too much to handle.

During the attack on Nottawasaga, British Lieutenant Miller Worsley and seventeen men escaped and went to Mackinac by canoe. Finding the situation there to be critical, he formulated a plan to capture the American vessels. On September 1, McDouall sent Worsley and his party on four batteaux to carry out this mission. On the evening of September 3, Worsley approached the *Tigress* and was not sighted until he was only one hundred yards away. The Americans fired their cannon and muskets but they failed to stop the British from boarding the ship. This short battle resulted in two British and three Americans dead and the British in control of an American ship.

The next day the *Scorpion* dropped anchor a couple miles away from the *Tigress*. Still flying the American flag, the *Tigress* gave no indication that it was in hostile hands. On the following day Worsley approached the *Scorpion*, and before its commander Lieutenant Daniel Turner recognized the presence of the British, they were too close to be repelled. The British boarded the *Scorpion* and took command of the ship. The loss of these two vessels ended any hopes the Americans had for recapturing Fort Mackinac.

men joined the army hoping to escape this kind of labor and became quite disillusioned when ordered to perform these tasks.

Yet each deserter had his own personal reasons for leaving. Boredom with military life or hatred for an officer motivated some to leave the island. Many men made the decision to escape while drunk. Occasionally a man was too ashamed to face his officers and fellowmen because of some deed he had done. Rather than undergo embarrassment or a court-martial, he figured it was easier to run away. Some soldiers sought to avoid paying large debts they had incurred through gambling or borrowing. Frequently a man became acquainted with a woman and would follow her when she left Mackinac. Sometimes marriage resulted, and the thought of starting a family while in the army was unbearable. To prevent this situation from happening, Captain Greenleaf Goodale suggested that the army require that a man receive his commanding officer's permission before he could marry.

Whatever the reasons for desertion, the army severely punished deserters. Privates Antoine Roberts and Thomas Carty served the rest of their enlistments at hard labor upon conviction in 1819. They also paid the costs involved in their apprehension by having one half of their monthly pay withdrawn for a year. In the 1870's courts-martial handed out stiffer penalties to Mackinac deserters. The judges ordered one private to be jailed for two years at hard labor, to forfeit all pay due him, and to be dishonorably discharged from the army. Some officers felt these penalties were too clement and recommended prison terms as long as five years.

Sometimes nature could be more cruel than the military. In 1820 a Private Porter attempted to desert to Drummond Island, but was returned to the fort. He was not put in the guardhouse. Instead he went on sick call having frozen his feet. The post surgeon amputated both of them. Three years later, Private James Sheridan suffered a similar fate attempting to get to Drummond Island. He lost his left foot, much of his right foot, and his ears as a result of being frozen.

Considering that the garrison at Fort Mackinac usually consisted of only one or two companies, it appears that these men got into more than their share of trouble; but it is important to distinguish between civilian and military discipline. A civilian who cursed his boss and became boisterous after too much drinking might get fired or receive a black eye with no legal actions involved. On the other hand, a soldier almost certainly would be court-martialed and disciplinary action taken. The necessity to maintain order forced the military to clamp down on any breach of discipline. Also, military records list the court-martial proceedings, whereas much disorder among civilians was never recorded.

Despite this, a bothersome question arises as to why the army had so much trouble with members of its ranks. Certainly the reasons given

Company F, First Infantry inside Fort Mackinac, 1870. Courtesy – Clarke Library, Central Michigan University.

46

by Sellers and other officers account for many of the disciplinary problems. However, there were other contributing factors. Loneliness helps to breed discontent. Many men stationed at Mackinac missed their families and friends, and they turned to liquor as a substitute. When under the influence of alcohol, they could not exercise good judgment and frequently got into trouble. These men not only worked together, but they also lived together in the barracks. Their close proximity to each other cultivated personality conflicts and afforded many opportunities for differences between individuals to be exacerbated. When ill feelings reached the breaking point, trouble usually resulted. A man promoted to corporal or sergeant from the ranks might use his authority to make it rough on an old antagonist, thereby creating an ideal situation for insubordination or a refusal to obey orders.

Some of the men had a difficult time adjusting to the nature of life at Fort Mackinac, and many were unprepared to cope with the hardships generated by the extreme winter climate. Isolation, drudgery, and loneliness could produce a very unhealthy situation. When these conditions were thrust upon men of weak constitutions or bad character, it was not surprising that they had little respect for rules and regulations. Breeches of discipline required that the army punish the offenders; usually this retribution was swift and harsh. The officers had the responsibility to make sure that the army's regulations were observed by all military personnel. Maintaining good discipline among the troops was one important function performed by the officers. This was essential if the post administration hoped to keep the garrison under control and functioning effectively.

VI.

POST ADMINISTRATION

At all times the highest ranking officer stationed at Fort Mackinac commanded the post. The government relegated the responsibility for the garrison's welfare and safety to him. He made sure that discipline was maintained, that the books were kept in order, and that provisions were given to the men. To assist him, the commandant assigned the other officers to supervise the functions of the various departments, such as the quartermasters, and to look after the details of everyday activities at the post. As a result the fort's administration involved the working together of the several officers and non-commissioned officers, but the final authority rested with the post commander. Throughout the years the nature of his job changed little until the creation of the national park. Then he became the park superintendent as well.

The length of command varied from a few months to several years. Whenever a new commander arrived, he went through some routine procedures. Beginning with Lieutenant Governor Sinclair, each succeeding commandant thoroughly inspected the physical condition of the fort's buildings and walls. Usually, the outgoing commander mustered the troops, at which time they were introduced to their new leader and reviewed. The new commandant also demanded that written reports be made regarding the quantity and quality of all goods in the storehouses. The post surgeon was directed to make an accounting of all medicines, surgical instruments, and hospital supplies on hand. Generally the books were presented for examination. All of this was necessary because the commanding officer was responsible for all the equipment and stores issued to his command. If the previous commander or any of his officers had been careless or dishonest, it was important that the new man discover this before assuming command of the post.

Upon his arrival the new commander sought to establish rapport with his troops. Sometimes this might be accomplished through a verbal greeting or favorable review of the troops. On other occasions, more dramatic devises were employed. Several days after taking charge in October, 1804, Lieutenant Colonel Jacob Kingsbury released all the prisoners in the guardhouse. Despite this leniency, he warned his men they could expect punishment for any misbehavior of which they were found guilty by a court-martial.

Generally there was no question regarding the chain of command. However in August, 1780 Captain John Mompesson of the King's Eighth Regiment arrived with a sergeant, a corporal, and twenty privates. Upon his appearance, he refused to recognize Sinclair as the commanding officer. Mompesson claimed that he had held his captaincy longer than Sinclair; consequently he should be in charge of the garrison. Although Mompesson's men assisted in the moving and construction of the fort, they looked to him as their commanding officer, not Sinclair. This split in the ranks divided the allegiance of the troops, and created confusion

Captain Greenleaf A. Goodale, Twenty-third Infantry, March, 1886.

among the civilians as to who was really in control. This matter was not cleared up until General Haldimand ruled in Sinclair's favor. Fortunately, this situation did not arise again.

The outcome of international events sometimes created uncertainty in a commander's mind, causing him to act without authorization from his superiors. Following the American Revolution, Captain Daniel Robertson feared that the British would have to leave after the war's end. To be prepared for this possibility, he began to make plans for constructing fortifications at Thessalon on the northern shore of Lake Huron. Although he had not received authorization, he sent several men there to locate a site and to begin cutting timber. When Haldimand learned of these activities, he ordered a halt and instructed Robertson to return all tools and iron works to Michilimackinac. Haldimand informed Robertson the following year in October that he need not fear the Americans, who were too weak to pose a threat, and that the British had no intention of leaving the post at that time. He obeyed Haldimand's orders and dropped his plans.

If any commandant was going to be successful, he had to have the cooperation of the other officers, as these men had to carry out the orders given to them. They made sure that firewood was being cut, that the troops were being drilled properly, and that sufficient supplies were obtained to keep the men alive and healthy. To accomplish this, the officers delegated most of these responsibilities to the non-commissioned officers, who made sure every man did his part. Also, each officer took his turn as officer of the day, being in charge of the guard and of the routine activities in the fort for a twenty-four hour period.

Officers had various responsibilities regarding Indian relations and trade. Although American commanders were not as deeply involved in Indian trade as their British predecessors, they checked traders' licenses when they stopped at Mackinac. When large numbers of Indians came to the island to exchange their furs for goods, a detail of troops stood guard to prevent disturbances that might be caused by too much liquor. After the Treaty of 1836 the Indian Dormitory was built as a place where Indians would receive payment and conduct any other business they had with the government. Between 1838 and 1846 they came to Mackinac in August or September to get their annual payment. A gunshot fired at the fort signalled the opening of payments, and the Indians made their way to the agent. Island merchants eagerly awaited this annual event because they were anxious to relieve the Indians of their funds. To protect the Indians while on government land, the commandant sent a detail to the dormitory to keep the merchants away. Once the Indians left the premises of the Agency, they found themselves at the businessmen's mercy. Many of them spent their money shortly after they received it.

50

Occasionally an officer led a party of men on government business to places quite a ways from Mackinac. In September of 1846 Captain Silas Casey of C Company, Second Infantry, ordered Lieutenant Fred Steele to go to LaPointe on Lake Superior. Steele and his three men were to watch over the payments being made to Indians there. Casey instructed Steele to work closely with the Indian agent so that the government business might be expedited as quickly as possible. The mission lasted about three weeks.

On some occasions when a private contractor supplied goods to the government, the commandant created a board to inspect the goods. These panels were usually composed of one officer and one prominent citizen of the village. Such individuals as Edward Biddle and Robert Stuart, from the American Fur Company, were called upon to verify the fulfillment of a contract. The commander authorized payment if the board was satisfied with the supplier's product.

When only one company was garrisoned at the post, the company commander was the post commandant. Any commander was held responsible for ordnance and stores issued to him. The most challenging job he had was to keep his men content and well disciplined. If a man's uniform was dirty or messy or his musket or rifle was rusty, the captain saw that the situation was corrected. He conducted weekly inspections of his men's quarters in addition to the weekly review on the parade grounds. The *Army Regulations* called for a company to be divided into four squads with each having a non-commissioned officer in charge. These sergeants and corporals usually made sure their men had clean bedding, pressed uniforms, and weapons in working order. Since the non-coms lived in the barracks, they kept a close watch over the men's personal habits. If their troops were sloppy or unkept, they would have to answer to their commander.

Due to the small size of the garrison, most officers drew extra duty assignments. Lieutenant Will Daugherty served as paymaster and quartermaster in 1875; for a time he was also the company and post commander while Captain Charles Dickey was absent on leave. Daugherty saw to it that supplies and men needed by the garrison were delivered to the fort. On pay days, which came at least every two months, he was quite popular as he had charge of the payroll. At the same time Lieutenant John McA. Webster filled in as post adjutant and recruiting officer. He took the morning roll call and read any orders for the troops from the commandant. In addition he handled most of the commander's correspondence and supervised any clerks who were employed copying and writing letters.

If there were enough officers present, the highest ranking two or three next to the commandant formed the Council of Administration. This organization met at least once every two months. As long as a

Dwight L. Kelton.

sutler was in business, the council determined the quantity and type of of goods he could stock. They examined his books, making sure no soldier was in debt more than he was able to pay. They also set the prices the sutler could charge and investigated any charges that his prices or practices were unfair. The council also fixed the rates charged by the company laundresses and made rules regulating the school.

Not all monies spent by the army were provided directly by the government. Both the post fund and the company fund were created to supplement needs not covered by regular appropriations. At Fort Mackinac these two funds were combined into one account when only one company was at the fort. Some cash for the post fund was generated through a tax on the sutler. This assessment could not exceed ten cents per man per month; the council set the exact fee. Another source of revenue was to save flour. If less than the full ration was consumed, the value of the unused portion was credited to the post fund. When the post bakery was operating, the garrison could bake all of its own bread, thereby avoiding the cost of a civilian baker's services. The post treasurer administered this fund. He disbursed it for bakehouse expenses, school books for soldiers' children, and new books for the post library.

On the other hand, when a separate company fund was maintained, it came from excess monies in the post or regimental funds and from savings on company rations. If a unit ate less bread or beef than their rations provided, the money saved could be used to purchase items for the men's enjoyment. In 1890 the companies raised five hogs at the post stable and sold them for $85.32, which added to their funds. All of the company's officers composed the company council who determined what was to be acquired with the fund. Generally they purchased such items as games and books. They also might sponsor a dance or activity involving the troops and the community.

As part of his inspection, the Inspector General examined and evaluated the post administration. He inquired into the adequacy of clothing and rations to see if they corresponded to the regulations. He also wanted to know if the men were being paid on time. These things were very important because inadequate clothing or food and lack of pay could seriously undermine troop morale and performance. If such a situation did exist, the Inspector tried to determine whether it was the fault of the fort's commandant or the army's procedures and methods of moving necessary goods. Usually the administration at Fort Mackinac was given high marks. Colonel George Croghan noted that the regulations were being followed in 1831, but he also commented that articles of clothing issued to the men were insufficient for the climate.

Of all the non-commissioned officers, the ordnance Sergeant probably played the most unique role. His name did not appear on the roll of any company or regiment; rather the Adjutant General assigned him to a post and transferred him when necessary. Consequently when a unit left the fort, the ordnance sergeant remained. If he wanted to be reappointed after his enlistment expired, he applied to the Adjutant General's office for another term. Unless his commanding officer found him to be incompetent and stated so in writing, he usually kept his position. No soldier spent more years at Fort Mackinac than Ordnance Sergeant William Marshall.

Marshall came to the garrison in 1848 and was still active in the early 1880's. His duties involved caring for all cannon, arms, ammunition, and other military stores. Apparently his expertise and ability were appreciated by the long succession of commandants under whom he served. He witnessed more changes at the fort than any other soldier, particularly the expansion of the physical surroundings. After the garrison was vacated during the Civil War, he was the only regular army man stationed there. He was put under the direction of the Chief of Ordnance Departments and left in charge of all the military hardware and supplies that were kept in storage. For part of this time the Stanton Guards used the post and undoubtedly found Marshall quite helpful. When the post was reoccupied following the war, Marshall awaited the arrival of Company B of the Forty-third Infantry. Throughout the years that he was in charge of the fort he made out the monthly and quarterly returns for the post.

Whenever a unit got orders transferring it to another post, the administration found itself quite busy. All the company's property and equipment had to be accounted for and shipped. A concentrated effort was made to get the fort in proper order for the new unit. Besides these details, each man had to pack his and his family's personal possessions. When all of this was accumulated, it amounted to a lot of gear. In 1884 Companies C and D of the Tenth Infantry were assigned to Fort Union, New Mexico. This involved the removal and transporting of seventy-one men, eight wives, five servants, seven and one-half tons of company property, five and one-half tons of officers property, books, and papers, plus personal items belonging to the enlisted men.

The departure of soldiers often attracted considerable community interest. On May 8, 1890, two companies of the Twenty-third Regiment left Mackinac Island aboard the steamer *Algomah* for Mackinaw City,

The ALGOMAH.

where they took a train to San Antonio, Texas. A large crowd of villagers turned out to watch the men march down the hill to the dock and board the boat. For many soldiers and citizens this marked the parting of friends.

Occasionally, the post commander became involved in legal arguments with village residents regarding boundaries and uses of government property. In 1870 Captain Leslie Smith disputed Edward Franks right to use the old Mission House as a summer hotel. This building was located on government land that had been used by the American Board of Commissioners for Foreign Missions for an Indian mission between

54

1823 and 1837. Apparently Smith evicted Franks but shortly thereafter was ordered to let him return until the matter was resolved. Military correspondence revealed that the ABCFM had conveyed some buildings and land to Franks in 1855; but since the Board did not own the land, they could not have given Franks legal title to it. Following much correspondence and a survey of the land, Congress empowered the Secretary of the Treasury to sell the land surrounding the Mission House to Franks.

The commandant was responsible for caring for the post cemetery. He saw that markers were erected after the burial of a soldier. Since cattle sometimes roamed in the area of the graveyard, fences had to be maintained to keep them out. The garrison also kept the flag flying over the cemetery. In 1884 Captain George K. Brady got involved in a project to improve the condition of the adjacent Protestant Cemetery. A number of local residents believed it to be a "disgrace" and sought to erect a fence to keep out the cattle. The cost of $250 was to be met through contributions from persons who had relatives buried there. Brady was asked to help solicit the money by writing to these people asking for contributions and explaining the need for the fence.

Another matter that the commandant had to deal with was personnel problems. Leslie Smith, a stickler for detail, became very unhappy with the post surgeon, Captain William M. Notson, in August of 1873. Smith charged that Notson spent more time at the Mission House and "in a low grog shop in the village" than he did practicing medicine. Smith felt that he was a bad example for his men and cited a marked increase in drunkenness at the post during the previous three months. Smith succeeded in having Notson relieved of his duties. Whereupon Notson accused Smith of using a soldier to groom his horse and keeping it in the government stable. Smith replied that he did this at his own expense, employing the soldier during his free time for five dollars a month.

Notson, feeling little love for Smith, found another way to irritate him. On a Sunday afternoon Notson was drinking in a village saloon. Some of the enlisted men were present and became the recipients of his generosity. He ordered the bartender to supply all the liquor that these men wanted at Notson's expense. To his delight two of them got quite drunk, began fighting outside the barroom, and were arrested. Needless to say, Smith was infuriated and reported the incident to the Adjutant General's office, though he did not prefer any new charges. Although Notson was soon transferred, his episode with Smith apparently did not interfere with his military career. In July, 1879, he was appointed to the Army Medical Examining Board in New York City. He died on June 23, 1882, at Columbus Barracks, Ohio, from "nervous prostration."

In the summer of 1883 a disagreement arose between Lieutenant Dwight L. Kelton and his commander Captain Edwin Sellers. Kelton had written a book describing the legends and history of Mackinac Island and was selling it to summer visitors. For some reason, Sellers ordered him to remove all signs advertising the *Annals of Fort Mackinac* from the national park and military reservation, and he forbid Kelton from selling any copies on government property. These orders were put in writing, as Seller's earlier verbal commands had been ignored by Kelton. Shortly after Seller's death on April 8, 1884, his successor, Captain Charles L. Davis removed all restrictions on the *Annals*.

After the formation of the Mackinac Island National Park in 1875, the commandant also served as the park superintendent. To help perform the extra labor required by the park, the commander and Senator Thomas W. Ferry both requested that another company be stationed at Mackinac. Additional manpower was needed to maintain the park and to construct new facilities for visitor use. The garrison had to police the park to carry out the Congressional directive that the public not harm the island's resources, plant life, and wildlife. Also, the superintendent was authorized to utilize the park for military purposes, but he had to ensure the public's safety whenever such use was made. To help carry out this mandate, the army sent one more company of troops to Mackinac which helped to stimulate a large scale building program within the post.

As the park superintendent, the commandant faced many interesting and difficult problems which often required skill and diplomacy to resolve. Since the park's purpose was to provide for the public's well-being, it was important that the resources not be misused. One way this happened was through the unauthorized cutting of trees. In June, 1885, Captain George K. Brady learned that timber had been cut despite published warnings that this was illegal. Some soldiers apprehended Henry Paro and Antoine Truckey while cutting trees. Brady desired that they be prosecuted for this alledged violation. Fortunately he tempered his zeal by conducting a further investigation which revealed that no violation had occured. These two men were not within the park boundaries when they sawed down the trees. Other people irritated the superintendent by stripping bark off white birch trees. It was virtually impossible to locate these offenders.

Due to the island's beauty and ideal summer climate, certain wealthy people wanted to spend all or part of their summers there. As a result they sought to lease lots on government property, particularly along the picturesque east and west bluffs. The War Department was more than willing to oblige since any revenue produced could be used to improve the park. In fact, this usually was the only way the superintendent could get money for that purpose. He leased lots to prominent citizens of Michigan and the midwest for the expressed purpose of constructing summer dwellings. The first leases granted in the mid-1880's were for ten years and stipulated that a cottage must be built within one year or the lease would be forfeited. In an effort to encourage the leasing of more lots, tenants were given two years to build in 1887. The annual rent was twenty-five dollars. The post quartermaster reported that by the end of 1886 four cottages had been erected. Within the next few years many more would be constructed. The superintendent not only granted the leases, but he made sure that the lessees fulfilled their obligations. If they reneged, he cancelled their leases.

One of the major work projects in the park was the construction of fences. The men built a five-foot board fence around Robinson's Folly in 1878. This was needed to prevent unsuspecting visitors from exploring the potentially dangerous landmark and taking an unexpected tumble. New fences were also erected around the post cemetery and the post gardens to keep people from roaming freely through these restricted areas.

The soldiers undertook other projects for the benefit and safety of an increasing number of tourists. In 1886 Captain Greenleaf Goodale ordered his work crew to construct an observatory on Fort Holmes Hill. This twenty-foot tower gave visitors a majestic view of the Straits of Mackinac from the island's highest point. It cost $160 and was financed from the land rentals. Goodale's men built a handrail and laid planks over the pathway to Arch Rock. This, too, made the island's natural beauty more accessible to the public.

Visitors who hired carriage drivers to take them on a tour of the park helped pay for the upkeep of the roads. The village of Mackinac Island levied taxes on these operators for the purpose of maintaining good roads. This was quite important for local businessmen and tourists alike. Since government funds for park improvement were quite limited, it meant revenues had to be generated at the local level. If Mackinac Island was to be a significant tourist attraction, it was vital that visitors be able to enjoy it in comfort. Hence, an adequate road system had to be supported.

At times it became quite difficult to keep civilians out of areas reserved for military use. In May of 1878 Major Alfred L. Hough issued emphatic orders that the citizens were not to utilize the parade ground behind the fort. This field was reserved for exclusive use by the soldiers for military exercises and games. Any other person wanting to use it must first secure special permission from the commanding officer. Anyone who violated this regulation would be removed by the guard.

Another important function that the commandant carried out was to handle requests made by local residents and businessmen to make use of government property for private purposes. In 1884 James F. Cable asked permission to use water from the military reservation's spring, and he wanted to lay a pipe across the pasture to the John Jacob Astor House Hotel. This demand was granted upon condition that Cable put the pipe deep enough in the ground so it would not interfere with the pasture's normal use. He also agreed to remove the pipe whenever the government might think it desirable.

When the Grand Hotel or "Plank's Grand Hotel," as it was first known, was built, its owners also found it necessary to make use of public land. In the spring of 1888, the hotel's management built a livery stable to accommodate its horses. However, the stable was located on the other side of a twenty-foot strip of park land. The hotel requested and received

Two views of summer military encampments in the late 1880's on the U.S. Government pastures. Courtesy – Grand Hotel, Mackinac Island.

permission to cross this narrow sliver of ground. The problem of park boundaries and private use of government land created a number of problems that had to be carefully worked out to insure the best interests of all parties concerned.

The commanding officer had to make decisions as to where garbage would be dumped. Its proper disposal was necessary to prevent insects and rodents from breeding and creating a health hazard to the island community. He also had to decide how many interior and exterior lights needed to be lit throughout the night to ensure the safety of those residing in the park. He was responsible for the security of the park users, cottagers, and soldiers.

Although he had ample authority to make decisions, the post commander regularly communicated with his superiors. He reported significant incidents or problems to the Adjutant General. Frequently he wrote to the War Department asking for advice and information regarding the park and fort operations. When constructing new buildings, the post quartermaster received permission from the Quartermaster's Department to purchase materials. Through extensive correspondence the officers got authorization to make decisions and to acquire provisions necessary for the welfare of the garrison and government property. The most common means of communications was the mail. Except in winter, mail regularly left and came to the Mackinac Post Office, often containing military correspondence. By the late 1870's the fort made extensive use of the telegraph office located in St. Ignace. This enabled the post commander to relay and receive information on urgent matters more quickly than through the mails, which generally took a couple of weeks. During July, 1883 a cable was laid connecting St. Ignace and Mackinac Island, and the new telegraph station was only four hundred yards from the fort.

Throughout its history, Fort Mackinac was always quite accessible except during winter. Its location made it very easy to reach by water, despite its great distance from the major commercial centers of the country. All men and supplies came by boat with the exception of goods brought over on ice. However, by the early 1880's the railroads served northern Michigan. The army shipped provisions to Mackinaw City on the Grand Rapids and Indiana or the Michigan Central. Also, some goods arrived at St. Ignace on the Detroit, Mackinac, and Marquette. From these two places new troops and provisions were transported to the island by boat.

Administering Fort Mackinac was a complex assignment that required capable and honest men. The man in charge had to be able to work with his subalterns and to command the respect of his men. For the most part the commandants at the fort were of a high calibre. Despite many difficulties, they maintained discipline and kept the men adequately supplied with provisions. Most of the officers had a genuine concern for their men's health and happiness, and they sought to make life at the fort as comfortable as conditions would allow.

After Congress created the national park, the scope of the commanding officer's job broadened. Despite this, the post functioned as efficiently as it ever did, even though the size of the garrison increased. By this time the fort had little military significance, and the troops had little fear of any hostile activity. This, coupled with improvements in the garrison's facilities, due largely to the post administration's request, made Fort Mackinac quite comfortable. Life here was not always easy, but capable officers did much to relieve some of the hardships the men had to endure. It took a combination of the leadership of competent administrators and the cooperation of the troops to keep the garrison healthy.

Market Street, July 1856

VII.

SUSTENANCE

Whether it was summer or winter the men always needed food, clothing, and shelter. Though the army took great pains to insure that the basic needs of its soldiers were met, occasionally supplies reached very low levels. In order to provide diversity in their diet, the men gardened extensively and grew a great variety of vegetables. It was the quartermaster's responsibility to purchase sufficient amounts of meat, flour, and clothing. Whenever army rations or issues were inadequate, the men could supplement them with purchases from their small pay. Much of their money went into the hands of the post sutler.

Since most provisions had to be brought to the island from great distances, the quartermaster and commissioned officers tried to stock large quantities of food and clothing. This was absolutely necessary for the winter. Generally, thousands of rations of flour, dried vegetables, coffee, vinegar, sugar, salt, and canned meats were kept in the storehouse. Occasionally, the inventories got low, and the arrival of a boat loaded with supplies brought relief to the garrison. Not all food was consumed by the men, as dampness ruined many barrels of flour and sugar. In addition, the quartermaster frequently noted that goods had been damaged while being transported or through the carelessness of a soldier working in the storehouse. During times of shortages, wasted stores contributed to the curtailment of rations.

The army set the specifications for the basic daily ration, and it varied somewhat throughout the nineteenth century. The primary change was the addition of vegetables and the elimination of liquor. The *Regulations* in 1812 set each man's daily ration to include one and one-fourth pounds of beef or three-fourths pound of pork, eighteen ounces of bread or flour, one gill of rum, whiskey, or brandy, and lesser amounts of salt, vinegar, soap, and candles. The 1861 *Regulations* indicated that meat and flour allotments had not changed significantly, but each man was being fed beans or rice twice a week, potatoes and mixed vegetables. The War Department had stopped issuing liquor over thirty years earlier.

As the improved rations indicated, the military increasingly tried to upgrade the soldiers' diet. At Fort Mackinac this was done by having extensive post gardens, maintained on the ground below the fort. Soldiers supplied the labor needed to plant, to cultivate and to harvest the vegetables. Although during earlier years the kinds of plants grown were fewer, by 1886 a wide variety of vegetables were being planted. These included beans, beets, cabbage, carrots, corn, cucumbers, kohlrabies, lettuce, onions, parsnips, peas, radishes, squash, potatoes, tomatoes, turnips, and rutabagas. These not only varied the menu, but also contributed to the men's health. Any man, though he cursed the soil or hoe as he was weeding the garden, certainly was amply rewarded for his efforts at the mess table. On numerous occasions inspecting officers highly praised the gardens and complimented the garrison for raising "an abundant supply of vegetables."

Unfortunately nature sometimes interfered with the gardeners' best

Quartermaster's storehouse.

Cattle grazing on the government pasture.

efforts. A late or early frost could kill young seedlings and prevent growing plants from maturing. Also, insufficient or excess amounts of rain seriously hampered plant growth. Too much water and damp weather caused the potatoes to rot in the ground in 1887. Colonel George Groghan reported that in 1834 bad weather had wiped out the year's growth of vegetables. When this happened, everyone at the garrison suffered.

Fresh vegetables comprised a part of the diet on a seasonal basis, but meat had to be served all year. The quartermaster often had a difficult time locating reliable sources of fresh beef or pork. He was most happy when he could contract with a local supplier for weekly deliveries. During much of the 1830's, the post contracted with Michael Dousman for beef. When it was readily available, the men ate better meals. This was true in the 1870's when the troops heartily consumed rib roasts, steaks, and other prime cuts. As the supply of beef decreased, halfway through the next decade the soldiers found that their plates contained less meat, and it was generally of poorer quality. Instead of biting into a nice juicy steak, they sunk their forks and spoons into stews. If fresh beef could not be obtained, pork or salt beef might be substituted. Bacon was very popular, particularly because it could be preserved quite easily. Some fresh pork was purchased at times from local residents and suppliers, although salt pork was more generally obtained.

In an attempt to try to create a ready supply of meat, Lieutenant Daniel Curtis devised a plan in 1819 for raising cattle on Bois Blanc Island. He proposed that one hundred cows, one hundred breeding sows, and four yoke of oxen be located there. In addition, a detail of one officer, two non-commissioned officers and twenty privates would be stationed there to care for the animals. Curtis estimated that this would cost

63

$2,240, and would result in a substantial saving to the government. This outpost would be able to supply meat to the posts at Green Bay and Chicago as well as Mackinac. To his disappointment, Curtis's superiors were unimpressed with his creative suggestions.

Many of the men found their diets monotonous, particularly during the winter. However, outside observers felt that the soldiers ate quite well. Croghan said in 1833 that the men lived and ate better than most island residents. The army's meals of salt meats, fish, fresh beef and vegetables provided adequate nourishment for each soldier. All of this food was prepared in the post kitchen by several enlisted men under the direction of a non-commissioned officer.

The kitchen hummed with activity, as it was a sizable task to feed fifty or sixty men or more each day. Each private in the company was required to take a regular turn. This duty could be quite unpleasant as it was often hot and tedious. Peeling potatoes or preparing stew was monotonous and boring. Army regulations stipulated that soups be cooked at least five hours and all vegetables be soft and digestable. When bread was baked at the post bakery, the privates kneaded the dough and put it into the oven. Before any bread could be eaten, it had to be cold. The mess crew's job did not end with food preparation, since all dirty dishes, pots, and utensils had to be washed. The commanding officer or company commander made frequent inspections of the kitchen to ensure that all regulations were being observed. The sergeant or corporal in charge had to make sure no unauthorized persons entered the kitchen and to prod his crew to sweep the floors and to clean off table tops in the mess hall. Cleanliness and orderliness were two standards that had to be constantly upheld in the kitchen.

The troops ate their heaviest meals in the morning and at noon. Breakfast might include bacon or salt pork or perhaps whitefish or trout along with bread and coffee. After a morning of fatigue and drill, the soldiers ate a dinner of beef roast or stew, potatoes or rice, perhaps some soup, along with bread and coffee or tea. During the summer fresh vegetables usually supplemented this menu, and dried vegetables and beans were added during the rest of the year. The evening meal often consisted only of bread and coffee.

If a man desired foods not served at the mess hall, he was able to obtain additional victuals at the commissary. It was here that family men purchased groceries for their wives and children. The commissary stocked numerous articles in addition to the regular rations. In 1877, the post surgeon noted that candles, canned vegetables and cornstarch had been purchased. Milk, cream, butter and eggs were also available. The men discovered that their small pay allowance did not stretch very far when buying milk at thirty-two cents a gallon, cream at forty cents per quart, butter at thirty-five cents per pound, and eggs at forty cents per dozen.

Those desiring an occasional chicken or turkey dinner were apt to be disappointed, as the commissary officers had a difficult time buying any poultry.

Stocking large quantities of foodstuffs required adequate storage facilities. On several occasions the post commander expressed great concern regarding this matter and seldom had any difficulty getting authorization to build a new storehouse when needed. The cost of ruined flour and other goods was far greater than that of a new building. For years the provisions storehouse stood at the bottom of the hill near the waterfront. This location made it easy to move goods from supply boats to the storehouse, but difficult to transport the rations to the kitchen. In 1819 a new structure was erected to house the 50,000 rations already at the fort and the large quantities that were still to be shipped. After the new hospital was built in 1859, the old hospital served as a provisions storehouse. The present commissary was constructed in 1879. When the storage building was not large enough, the quartermaster utilized empty space in other buildings. In 1855, he had stacked bags of potatoes six feet high in the barracks basement. Large quantities of food were needed to survive the winter months.

The quartermaster also had the responsibility to keep clothes on the men's backs. Generally he was able to procure enough clothing to fulfill army regulations; however the army's uniform allowance did not always meet soldiers' needs in a cold climate. As a result, officers and men frequently complained that they needed more warm clothes. Each man received several caps or hats, one or two coats, three flannel shirts, two or three trousers and flannel drawers, four pair of boots and four pair of

The post gardens below Fort Mackinac. Courtesy – Clarke Library, Central Michigan University.

65

stockings each year. He was also issued one blanket during the first and third years of his five-year enlistment and one great coat upon enlistment. Major General Edmund P. Gaines recommended in 1824 that the troops in northern latitudes be issued another pair of boots and one more great coat. Mackinac's icy winds and snow quickly chilled a man whether on guard or chopping wood. Adequate clothing was essential to the garrison's health.

It was imperative that each man take proper care of his clothing. If he lost any article or wore it out before he was due to get a replacement, he had to purchase the new garment out of his pay. The officers required their troops to keep their uniforms clean and neat, as it was important that the men look sharp. Unkempt uniforms often indicated a sloppy attitude, and company commanders had little use for that. Fortunately, the men did not have to wash their own clothes because the army allowed each company to employ four laundresses. These women washed not only uniforms but also bedding and kitchen linens.

Throughout the fort's history the troops lived in the barracks and, on some occasions, in the blockhouses. Except for a short time after the War of 1812, when several hundred men were stationed at Mackinac, one or two companies occupied the garrison, usually only one. Although the size of a company varied, it generally consisted of between thirty-five and fifty men. During most of the national park era, two companies were present. Though barracks living was not luxurious, its accommodations were better than many cabins scattered throughout the countryside. Normally men of the same squad lived together. The wooden bunks accommodated four and sometimes six men. Due to the lack of heat, the men were able to keep warmer by sleeping together and sharing their precious blankets. Although a straw mattress was beneath them, the men found the bunks quite hard. Other barracks furniture included stoves, tables, and chairs or benches. Most men spent many off-duty hours in their barracks room.

If some quarters were better furnished than others, men with more seniority were given preference when assigning quarters. Consequently, recruits usually found themselves with the hardest bunks and poorest stoves. Seniority gave way to company location when more than one was present. The men of different companies rarely bunked in the same rooms.

During the week the post police made sure the barracks rooms were kept clean and fresh, but on Saturdays the men of the company engaged in housecleaning activities. Each squad leader made his men change their bedding, sweep the floors, scour the tables and benches, and dust off all other objects. All furniture and accessories had to be put in order, including the men's personal items. If everything was not in its proper place or things were messy, the company commander would certainly chastise his troops for their slothfulness.

66

No enlisted man became wealthy from his monthly pay. The army provided food, clothing and shelter for its enlisted men but did not give them much cash. In 1812 a private earned five dollars a month; sixty years later his monthly allowance had risen to the whopping sum of thirteen dollars. Corporals and sergeants received two or three dollars more each month. Officers did somewhat better. A captain's salary increased from $480 per year in 1812 to $1800 by 1881, while a 1st lieutenant's pay jumped from $360 to $1600 per year. Additional monthly pay was awarded for re-enlistment. The 1861 *Regulations* allowed each man a two dollar per month pay hike for re-enlisting and another dollar for each succeeding five-year hitch. The 1881 *Regulations* called for a one dollar per month increase for each of the last three years of a man's enlistment. Upon re-enlistment a soldier got the rate he was receiving after the fifth year of his first tour of duty. A private did not directly receive his entire pay, as two dollars from each month's wage was withheld. This was given to the man after his enlistment expired. During the last half of the nineteenth century, each man also contributed twelve and one-half cents per month to the Soldiers' Home in Washington, D.C.

When they got to the pay table, many soldiers saw a sizable chunk of their wages go to the post sutler. If a man was out of cash and needed some merchandise from the sutler, he could go into debt up to one-third of his monthly wage. When pay day arrived, the sutler was paid off before the soldier got his money. Since the army granted the sutler a monopoly on the post, he often came under severe criticism for overcharging and selling goods of inferior quality. To investigate these accusations whenever they arose, the commandant convened a board of officers to examine the sutler's records and wares. Such a board investigated the activities of John Dousman, the sutler in 1820, and found him to be operating in a fair manner, selling commodities of good quality at reasonable prices.

Sutlers stocked and sold a variety of goods that added to the comfort of the troops. Men who smoked or chewed made frequent trips to the sutler to purchase tobacco and clay pipes. A thirsty soldier could get a quick drink of whiskey or a bottle of beer at the store. Anyone desiring to write to friends and family purchased paper, pens, and ink from the sutler. He also peddled such necessities as razors, knives, fish hooks, tooth brushes, spices, and a host of other items that a soldier might find useful. A good sutler made an effort to carry products that the men at the post needed and wanted. Not only did this keep the men content, it helped his business.

Life at Fort Mackinac entailed very few luxuries. The real challenge was to provide adequately for the men's basic physical needs. The army expended considerable effort to acquire ample rations and clothing. It was expensive to transport provisions to this distant post, but it was necessary. Although the troops usually received their regulation uniform allowances, this was not always enough in the cold climate. Inadequate clothing, coupled with rather chilly barracks, created some discomfort during the winter, yet the men survived. To sustain themselves the men at the garrison had to work hard to grow vegetables and to build their quarters. Their small pay left them with very little money to satisfy more than their most immediate needs and desires.

Soldiers leaving Fort Mackinac for new assignment. Courtesy—Michigan State Archives.

VIII.

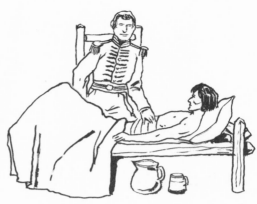

SICK CALL

The men of the garrison often needed medical assistance. Arduous tasks and extreme climate subjected them to frequent illness and injury, treatment of which was the duty of the post surgeon. Despite limited facilities and lack of modern medical knowledge, these doctors did much to keep the troops and the villagers healthy.

Although these physicians were usually officers, sometimes civilian doctors were employed. They assumed the responsibility to safeguard the physical well-being of the entire island community since the availability of doctors on the island was limited. Frequently the army surgeon petitioned his superiors for permission to establish a private practice. Dr. William S. Comstock made such a request to the Surgeon General in 1819 saying there was no citizen physician in the village and, "The inhabitants occasionally are in need of medical aid." While such a practice certainly would be financially beneficial to the individual doctor, it was necessary for the well being of the citizens and the soldiers.

The sick and wounded were cared for in the post hospital. Before 1828 the hospital facilities were quite crude. An old storehouse served as the first medical building. When requesting a replacement in 1824, Dr. William Beaumont lamented that the present structure was "cold and smoky in the winter" and that it "leaked rain in the summer." His successor, Dr. Richard S. Satterlee, also complained that the conditions were not conducive to convalescence. Despite this situation, Colonel George Croghan praised the work of Beaumont in such an unfit building. In 1826, Croghan described the building as a "perfect barn in ruins and so open at the top that during a rain the bunks of the patients are moved from place to place to avoid the wet." Certainly his reports helped bring about the construction of a new hospital in 1827.

Some of the most important experiments in the study of human digestion took place in the dilapidated old quarters. A young voyageur, Alexis St. Martin, received a severe gunshot wound at the American Fur Company's retail store located just below the fort. Immediately following the incident witnesses summoned Dr. Beaumont to the store to attend to St. Martin. Believing that young Alexis would not live, Beaumont treated his wounds and left him in the store. Upon his return several hours later,

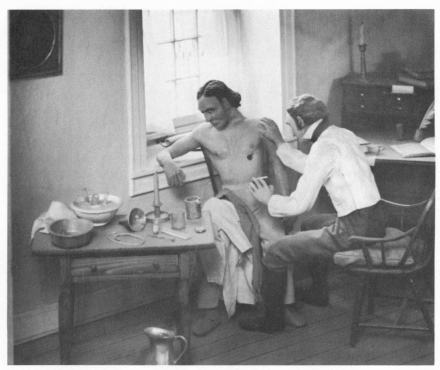

Diorama depicting Dr. William Beaumont treating Alexis St. Martin.

Beaumont discovered his patient still alive. He then ordered St. Martin removed to the post hospital, where he carefully ministered to his wound. To Beaumont's surprise, St. Martin lived, but the wound to his stomach never closed. This afforded a unique opportunity to observe the process of digestion. Being a keen and inquisitive young surgeon, Beaumont conducted a series of experiments upon his patient. The results of these experiments were published in 1833 as the *Experiments and Observations on the Gastric Juice and the Physiology of Digestion*. Beaumont's work represented a pioneer effort in man's understanding of his own digestive process.

70

Although Beaumont recommended the construction of a new hospital below the hill, his advice was not heeded. Apparently he felt that such a location would be more accessible to the inhabitants than the present site. Undoubtedly his experience with St. Martin and other civilians convinced him of this. The new hospital was built on the present foundation in 1827, burned, and was rebuilt in 1828. This structure served as the hospital until 1859, when a new and larger one was built just east of the fort.

While Beaumont gained great fame for his work at Mackinac, most of the post surgeons' work went unnoticed beyond the island. Soldiers went on hospital call for a wide variety of illnesses. The climate at times proved quite disagreeable to the troops. Frequent cases of catarrh and bronchial ailments caused much discomfort and were aggravated by the cold and humid air. When afflicted, a soldier would usually spend several days in bed under the surgeon's watchful eye.

Another frequent type of illness was stomach and bowel disorder. Diarrhea and dysentery occasionally struck soldiers and villagers in epidemic proportions. In 1887 many island residents and visitors suffered from such an outbreak. Dr. Charles Woodruff traced the cause of the disorders to impure drinking water. The town pump was located on the "inner end of the dock" near waters described as "maybe stagnant." Woodruff observed that there was little current at this place in the bay. He also noticed that vessels emptied their water closets nearby and that the water surface was covered with debris thrown in by nearby residents. To add to the pollution, the town drainage poured into the bay near the town pump. The epidemic spread to the garrison after its pump broke down and drinking water was fetched from Haldimand Bay. When some soldiers reported sick, Woodruff ordered all water used for human consumption to be dipped from a spring. Even this water was suspect because the fort's drainage might be seeping into the spring. He recommended that a new tile sewage system be installed at the fort. Within two years this was accomplished.

The surgeon was alert for killer diseases such as typhoid and cholera. An outbreak of such diseases could decimate the island's population. Scattered cases were reported from time to time, but the work of the doctor usually helped prevent serious epidemics. Yet, the island was not immune to these killers. The summer of 1832 saw cholera spread from Quebec to Montreal to the western lake region. In late June it arrived at Mackinac, threatening all the soldiers, fur company clerks, mission family, and village inhabitants. The disease also endangered the lives of over a hundred troops that had stopped at Mackinac, bound for Chicago. Apparently, decisive measures were taken to protect the garrison as the Post Returns for June and July indicate that only three men were on sick call. By mid July the cholera had moved on.

71

Many of the men's medical problems resulted from their own actions. A soldier who tasted too much whiskey might have to be treated for inebriation. He was allowed "to dry out" in the hospital, generally to the great displeasure of his commander. Others who took fancy with some of the local women sometimes found themselves infected with syphilis or the "clap." Improper eating and drinking habits contributed to numerous cases of constipation.

Injuries, too, caused considerable pain. Since much of the work done by troops was dangerous and required the use of tools, accidents frequently occurred. Cuts, bruises, gunshot wounds, burns, and broken bones had to be treated. In January, 1886, due to a heavy snowfall, a detail of soldiers was ordered to clear snow off the roofs of fort buildings. While carrying out this assignment, Private Peter Mitchell climbed on top of the officers' quarters and began shovelling snow. Unfortunately he slipped and fell, dislocating both bones of his left forearm. Within an hour Dr. John R. Bailey had reduced the dislocation, the necessary operation being performed while Mitchell was under a chloroform anaesthesia. Not all injured men were as fortunate. Dr. Beaumont cared for a Private Shaw in late 1820. Apparently Shaw got involved in a scuffle and his opponent hit him over the head with a heavy club, breaking his skull. After several weeks' treatment, Shaw finally died.

One of the most difficult problems confronted by physicians during the early nineteenth century was the relief of pain. William Beaumont knew two plants which produced drugs that could be used to treat the

Interior of post hospital.

sick. He grew both *papaver somniferum,* which produced opium, and *marribium vulgare,* which produced horehound. Usually when these drugs were given, the suffering patients experienced some relief. On a cold, dark November evening in 1822, Private James Randall fell while walking his post and broke his leg. To help ease his pain, Beaumont gave him a small opium pill. Beaumont also noted that opium and horehound were most effective in treating pulmonary ailments.

Besides the personal discomfort accompanying sickness and injury, many work days were lost to the army. For the year 1882, the surgeon treated 113 cases of illness resulting in a total of 1,337 days lost. The number of men garrisoned at the fort during this year ranged from fifty-six to seventy-seven. This means that approximately five per cent of the total number of soldier days were spent in the hospital.

The surgeon actively practiced preventive medicine. Besides being on the lookout for stagnant water, he attempted to locate spoiled foods which caused digestive disorders. In this matter, he got help from the quartermaster in making sure that beef and fish were indeed fresh. Rancid meats not only made soldiers sick, but made them quite unhappy as well. Sometimes food eaten in the village caused problems for citizens and soldiers alike. The doctor also encouraged the growing of fresh vegetables to improve the men's diet. Any measures that could be taken to prevent illness helped to strengthen the morale of the troops.

In the mid-1870's Dr. J. V. DeHanne deplored the condition of the post privies. Excepting the ones at the commanding officers' quarters and the hospital, they were all in "bad condition." The facilities at one location were described as "vile and intolerable: They are in immediate proximity to the kitchens, almost opening into them." With this obvious health hazard, DeHanne demanded that work begin, as soon as weather permitted, to change the situation. Certainly warm temperatures would have contributed to the breeding of germs and filth-carrying insects.

Dr. Bailey combated disease in still another way, with an extensive vaccination program. In 1882 he examined eighty-nine people and found that thirty-eight officers and men with twenty of their women and children needed vaccinating and were treated. Of this total, forty-six were successfully immunized. Perhaps the other twelve had natural resistance to the small pox.

By 1880 the post doctor, George W. Adair, had a sizable staff to assist him. Louis Pauly was the hospital steward. He saw that the patients were fed, properly bedded, and kept as comfortable as possible. He also supervised the work of the attendant and the cook. Considerable effort was expended to insure the comfort and well-being of the infirm.

Even though Fort Mackinac was somewhat remote from centers of medical activity, the post surgeon made an effort to keep informed of new practices and techniques. In the 1870's he subscribed to such jour nals as *American Medical Journal, Medical and Surgical Reports, Medical Times,* and *Medical Record.* He also maintained a professional library containing numerous books describing various diseases, treatments, and surgical techniques. Through the study of such publications, it was possible for the doctor to keep informed of medical advances. Thus, when he treated the ill and injured, he put to use the discoveries of others. For the patient, this could mean less pain and quicker recovery.

When the doctor could not be quickly reached in emergencies, the officers or enlisted men would have to treat a fallen comrade. In an effort to prepare the men for such a situation, the surgeon delivered medical lectures from time to time. In the spring of 1888, Dr. Woodruff gave a series of twelve lectures on administering first aid. Quick and proper action could save a life or a limb. Hence the troops were instructed on treating various types of wounds resulting from accidents with firearms and tools. Woodruff prescribed treatment for fevers and sudden illnesses. While soldiers stationed at Fort Mackinac did not normally expose themselves to combat situations, they might find themselves fighting Indians in the west when their company was transferred. As a result, knowing how to care for a gunshot or arrow wound could make the difference between life and death.

Despite his best efforts, the surgeon occasionally lost a man to the hand of death. A fever that could not be broken might cause a man to succumb. Alvan L. Bates battled an intermittent fever compounded by pneumonia for four weeks before he expired on June 13, 1874. Others died from respiratory and digestive ailments. Death was no respecter of rank and age. On April 8, 1884, post commander Captain Edwin E. Sellers died after a lingering illness. Sellers and Bates were buried in the post cemetery. Approximately 140 soldiers and members of their families are interred there. Of these graves only 107 are marked and only thirty-four can be identified.

When a soldier, a prominent local citizen, or an important government official died, the garrison paid proper respects. Captain Joseph Gleason of the Fifth Infantry passed away in late March, 1820. His military funeral involved all the officers and off-duty troops. Captain Benjamin K. Pierce commanded the escort to the post cemetery, with four of Gleason's fellow officers serving as pall bearers. Since there was no chaplain or Protestant clergyman on the island, Dr. Comstock assumed the role of chaplain. Prominent citizens, invited to participate in the procession, took their places behind the officers as they took Gleason's remains to the cemetery, where he was interred the day after his death.

Retired officers also received a formal military funeral. Captain Edwin C. Gaskill, who had served at Fort Mackinac in the late 1860's, returned to Mackinac Island in 1870. He became a prominent citizen in the community, serving as Village President for two years. During the Civil War he had lost his right arm, which caused him problems for the remainder of his life. Upon his death in 1889, the civilians and soldiers accorded him full honors. Services were held at the Episcopal Church below the fort. Then a full company of Regulars under arms, accompanied by the island cornet band, escorted the flag-draped casket to the fort cemetery. After graveside proceedings, the troops fired three musket volleys. With the sounding of taps, Captain Gaskill was laid to rest.

The garrison paid tribute to deceased generals. All of the officers at the fort wore black crepe around their left arms and the hilt of their swords for thirty days in honor of General Anthony Wayne, who died late in 1796. To commemorate the death of important military figures, such as General William T. Sherman, the post flag flew at half-mast.

While death marked the end for some soldiers' existence, most of them were quite alive, and it was the post surgeon's job to keep deaths and illnesses to a minimum. His constant vigilance for the health of the garrison enabled him to spot hazards which might be corrected to prevent the outbreak of serious illnesses. The men developed a great dependence upon this man to pull them through their various ailments, and his successes added further to their respect for him. Most of the doctors who served at Fort Mackinac were not content with the knowledge they had acquired before their arrival. Rather, they made conscientious efforts to increase their medical understanding because this would make them better doctors. As a result, these men made a vital contribution to the well-being of the entire island community.

IX.

RECREATION

Soldiers living at Fort Mackinac spent their leisure time indulging in numerous types of amusement. Individuals took part in card games, chess matches, billiards, and many other activities. In later years the fort fielded a baseball team and a rifle team, which competed with challengers from the surrounding area. When holidays occurred, the garrison went to great lengths to observe the occasion properly. In the early 1800's the army made little effort to promote entertaining functions for its men, but by the 1880's the officers showed great interest in expanding recreational facilities.

Soldiers seeking entertainment went to the village, frequently visiting local saloons and establishments selling liquor. The camaraderie found in these places offered a pleasant change of pace from the military routine. It was here that the men learned the latest town news and gossip. When the fur traders came to the island, they gave the soldiers first hand accounts of their past year's experiences. By the middle of the century, the soldiers were swapping stories with the fishermen and sailors who happened to be in town. As more tourists and visitors began coming to Mackinac, the army men met them socially. Sometimes social drinking led to more than conversation and games; too much booze turned some men into troublemakers, resulting in fights and violent arguments. When this happened, the men involved usually had to account for their actions the next day.

Due to this problem, the commanding officer occasionally forbade his men from visiting the village or buying liquor from the town's merchants. In 1799 the commandant permitted the men to stroll through the village if in uniform, but he did not want to see them "in that low practice of skulking round every corner and running after engages for rum." Any man who got drunk was to be taken immediately to the guardhouse. Some men found it to be a real challenge to drink and stay out of trouble at the same time. Later efforts to limit the soldiers' use of liquor met with little success, since many men considered the use of alcohol an enjoyable and worthwhile experience. The army had no policy of prohibition, only a desire to curb intemperance. This was evident during some of the holiday celebrations.

Part of the commemoration of Independence Day in some years included issues of extra whiskey. On such days, fatigue duties and most military activities came to a halt. Generally the cannon fired a salute to the United States in honor of her successful Revolution. In the 1880's and 90's, the garrison took part in elaborate ceremonies with people of the village or St. Ignace. Both communities sought the assistance of the garrison in their celebrations because the presence of men in uniform added

Arch Rock. Courtesy – Kimball House Museum, Battle Creek, Michigan.

much glamour. In 1884, Captain George K. Brady refused an invitation to participate in the island's July 4th ceremonies because of a previous commitment to St. Ignace. On some occasions, the soldiers spent time in both places. For example, on Memorial Day, 1890 some of the troops, accompanied by the island cornet band, took a boat to St. Ignace to participate in proceedings honoring Americans killed in battle. Upon their return to the island, they marched to the cemeteries to pay their proper respects to the soldiers buried there.

Since many of the men were of Irish descent, St. Patrick's Day was a very special time. In 1805, Lieutenant Colonel Jacob Kingsbury issued orders that all Irishmen would be freed from duty in order that they might properly observe the day. Interestingly, all the troops except the Irish "were to be sober" on the 17th of March. In the interest of fair play, Kingsbury gave men of other nationalities a holiday on April 30th while the Irishmen performed garrison duties. Any who were among the Sons of St. Tammary were "permitted to have the music," and it was expected they would not disgrace the day by rioting and fighting.

On some occasions, the post commander extended his hospitality to his men. Kingsbury invited all of the ladies and gentlemen at the fort to have dinner with him on New Year's Day, 1805. Officers might also entertain enlisted men at special times, such as the commandant's birthday or during a visit by a dignitary. Gatherings like these helped boost the morale of the troops and improve relations between enlisted men and officers.

Most of the amusements usually involved only several men. Next to sleep, the men probably spent more of their spare time playing cards than doing anything else. Friendly games of cribbage or poker helped pass many hours. Men gathered around a table in the barracks, with the coffee pot on the stove, might lose much of their month's pay to a buddy. Gambling and card playing went together, and an unlucky player might find himself deeply in debt if he became reckless. When this happened, a man found it difficult to purchase tobacco and other such commodities which provided him with some enjoyment. Generally little money changed hands, however, since the men had very little of it.

While the card games might get quite noisy and boisterous, other contests tended to be more sedate. Serious minded soldiers avidly played chess, testing their skills against their buddies. Others challenged their comrades to checker games, also hoping to demonstrate their ability to dominate their friends in games of thought. These matches proved to be a welcome relief from the day's guard and fatigue duties.

Although many of the men read in the library, others brought their books to the barracks. Here they had an opportunity to exchange ideas and to argue politics, religion, women, or any other controversial subject. Coming from different backgrounds, it was not surprising that they

A soldier and his companion strolling through the park. Courtesy – Michigan State Archives.

held many different viewpoints. Not all of these discussions remained friendly or calm, as on a few occasions the guard intervened in disturbances instigated by disagreements over a card game or differences of opinion. Despite these incidents, the men enjoyed criticizing each other's convictions and prejudices.

Some men vented their feelings and emotions through music. They might play a mandolin or mouth organ while sitting on their bunks or the barracks veranda, often entertaining several others. While plucking the strings, the soldiers frequently sang. These songs and ballads told of the man's longing for a loved one or his home. In later years memories and legends of the Civil War were kept alive and passed on by the war ballad. Through singing and playing, a man released some of the emotional frustrations that army life generated. In addition, men expressed feelings of joy and happiness by singing.

As the army became more concerned about the marksmanship of its men, it sponsored competitive events for the sharpshooters. The officers selected men from the post to represent it at Divisional and Departmental meets. In 1885 Sergeant William Kiasbolling represented Company K and Private William Williams represented Company E of the Twenty-third Infantry at the Annual Rifle Competition at Fort Niagara, New York. These men were chosen on the basis of their success in shoot-offs with others at Mackinac. This was no small achievement, for forty-one men from the two companies had been awarded "Marksmen Certificates."

A year earlier the garrison put together a rifle team of ten men and officers to challenge the Cheboygan Rifle Team. On July 4th most of the garrison went to Cheboygan to watch their team in action. Out of a possible score of 510, the Mackinac marksmen scored 401 to Cheboygan's 385, thereby winning the silver cup selected as the prize. Later in the summer the Cheboygan team made a voyage to Mackinac Island hoping to gain possession of the cup. Again the soldier boys were victorious, this time by a score of 391 to 380.

One did not have to be a good shot to take part in team sports. Any fellow who could hit a curve ball or throw a good fastball would probably have made the fort baseball team. On the same days that the rifle team beat back the challenges of the Cheboygan shooters, Cheboygan's "Diamond Baseball Club" took the field against the post squad. The fort won the first game 17-10 and the twenty-five dollar prize. However, the Diamond Club defeated the soldiers in the return match. This did not make the garrison very happy, and they blamed the loss on the presence of three professional players added to Cheboygan's roster since the previous game.

During the later years of the nineteenth century, baseball became a very popular game with the soldiers. They regularly played teams composed of citizens of the village. In addition to the Cheboygan Club, they played teams from St. Ignace, Reed City, and elsewhere. Spectators who wished to watch these contests on the diamond behind the fort paid fifteen cents to get on the grounds and a quarter if they wanted to sit in the grandstand. Not only did these games boost troop morale and instill pride in them, but they provided entertainment for the villagers and tourists vacationing on the island.

The formation of teams reflected an attitude emphasizing the need for recreational activities on military posts. Throughout most of the 1880's, the post command sought more ways to create different types of healthy entertainment for the garrison. Due to the weather, outdoor activities were limited in winter. In 1886 Captain Greenleaf Goodale recommended that a gymnasium and a bowling alley be built. This facility would have served as a place where the men could exercise and compete in physical games, and it would have been used for drill and military maneuvers. Goodale also planned to install an indoor shooting gallery. Unfortunately, the army was unwilling to expend money on this project.

This lack of funds prompted Captain Jacob Smith to request permission to build boats in 1890. These small vessels were to be used for the benefit of both the fort and the park. Smith believed the exercise the men got from rowing would be quite healthy. Although this alternative to a gymnasium had merit, it did little to fill the need for wintertime recreation.

An enjoyable event involving both the garrison and the village was the post dance, which afforded an opportunity for the soldiers to entertain and meet some local girls. These festivities were probably held on the second floor of the barracks and later in the canteen. Music by both military and civilian musicians provided the accompaniment for the dancers. Certainly the soldier boys made their way to similar happenings in the village.

The officers hoped that increased leisurely activities would help to curb the high rate of desertion. This desire led to the creation of the canteen in the old officers wooden quarters in 1889. This building was divided into three large rooms. The first room had a bar and a lunch counter. The second housed a billiard table to be used for carom games, and the third had a fifteen-ball billiard table. Hence a large number of soldiers could be entertained in several different activities. At the bar, beer and light wines were sold. The commander saw to it that "the best and highest price beer — Schlitz of Milwaukee," was on tap. In order to raise money needed to keep the canteen open, beer sold at five cents for a big glass. Although coffee was served for several weeks, the demand was so slight that this practice was discontinued. The men's thirst for beer was far greater than for coffee. In addition to drink, the soldiers showed a fondness for sandwiches made of imported Swiss cheese, ham, and French mustard. The combination of these ingredients made a very sociable supplement to a soldier's bland diet.

In the other rooms more serious activities took place. The fort pool sharks challenged one another on the two billiard tables. The carom table had been purchased years before by some soldiers for seventy-five dollars, and the fifteen-ball table was ordered new from Chicago for $175. Men spent many enjoyable hours over these tables trying to best their buddies. On the new table alone, over forty dollars was made in a month at five cents a game. These areas also served as reading rooms where current newspapers and magazines were available. In the relaxed atmosphere, many of the men participated in games of chess, checkers, backgammon, cards, and dominoes.

Baseball field and grandstand behind Fort Mackinac.

81

Although the renovation of the building and most of the furnishings were paid for out of the company funds, some of the summer cottagers helped to make the canteen more pleasant. They provided piles of magazines, framed pictures, and many games. Henry W. Leman of Chicago donated a series of Civil War battle scenes and a bust of General John Logan that were put on display. Acts like this indicated the interest of the civilians on Mackinac Island in the garrison during the days of the national park.

Apparently the canteen helped improve the conduct of the men. It certainly helped keep them out of the village bars, as men could now drink their beer and play billiards closer to home. Having the men stay in the garrison made it easier to police their actions as well. If a man was drinking too much, he could be ushered to the barracks to sober up, hopefully without an incident. Also having a relatively inexpensive source of leisurely entertainment helped to make soldier life much more tolerable.

Another source of relaxation was the natural beauty of Mackinac Island. Men strolled around the island with their wives or girl friends, enjoying the romantic flavor of Mackinac's beaches, cliffs, and flowers. Exploring the interior acquainted them with the natural wonders unique to the island. They were inspired by the majestic view afforded at Fort Holmes or Arch Rock. They enjoyed associating Indian legends with such features as Sugar Loaf, Devil's Kitchen, and Chimney Rock. Although most soldiers did not view the island's topography this way, those who did found their spirits uplifted and refreshed.

To be happy, the men needed a well-rounded life. Recreation was one of the vital ingredients. Men who spent long days cutting wood, building fortifications and quarters, drilling, or guarding the garrison had to have a chance to relax. On the frontier, in a remote area, the opportunities were limited. Except for the observance of holidays or special events and maintaining a post library, the army did very little to provide for these needs until after the Civil War. The soldiers found their own recreation by drinking, singing, reading, and playing cards and other games. At times these activities got them into trouble.

However, keen officers recognized the needs of their men and made significant efforts to increase the range of ways the soldiers could spend their leisure time both profitably and enjoyably. Sometimes they entertained the troops and on other occasions they required them to take part in official celebrations. More importantly, men like Captain Goodale prodded the army to do more to make soldier life pleasant. He knew that activities such as those carried on in the post canteen would do much to boost the morale of the troops. Content soldiers made good soldiers. The men of the United States Army were going to drink, gamble, and make a lot of noise. It was the army's challenge to make sure this

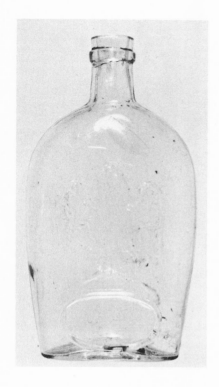

Whiskey bottle found at Fort Mackinac.

was done in such a way as to help the soldier and not get him into legal trouble.

The military also had the task of trying to involve its men in a number of activities. The formation of rifle and baseball teams not only included team members, but the rest of the garrison who intently watched the fate of their comrades battling against outsiders. Competition generated a new *esprit de corps* within the garrison and uplifted the men. As the recreational opportunities expanded, the men became more satisfied. This state of affairs prompted Captain Goodale to comment in 1886 that the men at Mackinac were "more contented than at any post I have ever seen." This had not always been true.

X.

MIND
AND SOUL

Although the soldiers spent most of their spare hours taking part in recreational activities, they did devote some time to exercises of the mind. Since most of the men could read, the army provided books and periodicals for the garrison. The military, at times, conducted classes whereby soldiers could improve their intellectual skills and acquire knowledge about subjects of interest. Classes were also held for the children of the men stationed at Mackinac. While considerable effort was made to stimulate and to satisfy the mental curiosities of the soldiers, the army provided opportunities for them to fulfill their spiritual or religious needs as well.

Throughout much of the nineteenth century the post maintained a library or reading room. As early as 1843, the Post Treasurer ordered a number of periodicals for the garrison. Upon their arrival, these publications were taken to the library and were made available to the men. Although the subscription list had only eight titles, a wide range of interests could be satisfied.

For those interested in controversial political questions, the *United States Magazine and Democratic Review* provided food for thought. Readers discovered that the *Democratic Review* took a non-equivocal stance on the deepening abolition crusade. Its neutral stance on the annexation of Texas tied in with its criticism of both the secessionists and the abolitionists. More viewpoints on national political questions were presented by the *National Intelligencer*. This daily gave an account of Congressional proceedings. In addition, it reported on many significant events that occurred throughout the country and the world. By reading these accounts, officers and men followed the development of such things as national political campaigns, the deepening crisis with Mexico, and the various reform movements.

The *Democratic Review* published more than political discussions; it also carried the works of some of the greatest contemporary writers. Authors such as William Cullen Bryant, Nathaniel Hawthorne, John Greenleaf Whittier, and Henry Wadsworth Longfellow contributed works for the magazine. Their poetry and stories reached the men at Mackinac by way of this magazine. Despite their great distance from the Northeast, men with literary tastes were able to enjoy the works of their favorite authors.

Soldiers who had an interest in sports or the stage faithfully read *The Spirit of the Times.* This magazine dealt primarily with the lighter side of life. It gave details of race meetings and published engravings of famous horses. It also devoted much space to the theater, enlightening its readers with the latest news about actors, actresses, and certain productions. From time to time, engravings of actresses appeared on its pages. This magazine introduced the soldiers to the various pieces of music it published.

Other publications received at the fort contained more ideas and information for their readers. *Albion* excerpted selections from foreign journals for its subscribers. The soldiers learned of military news and developments in the *Army and Navy Chronicle.* Several of the large eastern newspapers had extensive news coverage and numerous advertisements for new products. *The Philadelphia Inquirer, The New York Herald,* and *The New York Express* kept men who were from the East informed of what was going on in their home states. The men learned the results of sporting events, elections, and business news in addition to hundreds of other items.

By the mid-1880's some of the titles received had changed, but the men still had similar interests. Now they were reading such publications as the *Century, Harper's Weekly, Harper's Monthly, Frank Leslie's Popular Monthly, Frank Leslie's Illustrated* and *Puck.* While their predecessors read Hawthorne and Whittier, the men of the eighties read the work of such authors as Henry James, Mark Twain, and William Dean Howells in *Century.* Its editors had serialized James' *The Bostonian* and Howells' *The Rise of Silas Lapham* among other significant works. One interesting piece that appeared in *Century* in 1885 was an episode from the then unpublished "Adventures of Huckleberry Finn." In addition, short stories and poetry regularly appeared in *Century* and *Frank Leslie's Popular Monthly.* While most soldiers probably did not have a great interest in poetry, F. M. Newton's "Taps," which appeared in *Century* in 1885, commemorating the death of General Ullyses S. Grant, must have had a very special meaning for any Civil War veteran who happened to read it.

"Brave heart, good-night, the evening shadows fall;
Silenced the tramping feet, the wailing dirge,
The cannons' roar; faint dies the bugle call,
'Lights out!' — the sentry's tread scarce wakes the hush,
Good-night.

"Swift flows the river, murmuring as it flows, —
Soft slumber-giving airs invite to rest;
Pain's hours of anguish fled — tired eyelids close —
Love wishes thee, as oft and oft before,
Good-night.

"The stars look down upon thy calm repose
As once on tented field, on battle eve;
No clash of arms, sad heralder of woes,
Now rudely breaks the sleep God's peace enfolds, —
Good-night.

"Thy silence speaks, and tells of honor, truth,
Of faithful service, — generous victory, —
A nation saved. For thee a nation weeps, —
Clasp hands again, through tears! Our Leader sleeps!
Good-night."

Poems such as this made up only a small part of the literature written about the Civil War during the following decades. Many veterans and recruits alike took great interest in articles like the "Capture of Fort Donelson," or "Recollections of a Private," that appeared in 1885 in *Century*. Many authors wrote countless other accounts about famous battles, incidents, and soldiers. It was not surprising that the army subscribed to periodicals that stirred memories of the war.

Many of the articles appearing in these periodicals enlightened the men regarding advances in science and technology. *Frank Leslie's Popular Monthly* had a number of scientific essays. The *Century's* "Open Letter" department carried reader's opinions and ideas on a wide range of interests, particularly science. They discussed electrical progress, advances in communication, archaeology, mechanical innovations, and numerous other topics of current interest. Since this was a time of rapid technological change, it was likely that some of the men developed interests in new innovations. Many times new inventions, such as pumps and lighting devices, might have practical applications at the fort.

Some writers, particularly the editor of *Century*, pricked the consciences of their readers. In his "Topics of the Time," he discussed a number of moral issues and questions. A few of these applied directly to habits and attitudes held by army men. Personal abuses and excesses were discussed. Men were criticized, especially the poor, for being imprudent in their personal business, implying that this contributed to their poverty. Subscribers read some biting comments about individuals who defaulted on their debts or who took marriage vows too lightly. Editorialists, also, expressed critical viewpoints on such phenomena as the women's suffrage movement, temperance crusades, and religious affairs. Many soldiers enjoyed the jabs *Puck* made at political corruption and other institutional abuses.

As cities west of the Appalachians grew, the post subscribed to newspapers from places other than the East. At different times during the 1880's, the *Chicago Times, Chicago Tribune, Detroit Evening News* and *Detroit Free Press*, along with various New York papers, all found their way into the library. Soldiers could watch closely the happenings of the growing sport of baseball, the winners of horse races, and the results of prize fights. They also learned of the economic and political problems facing the country. *Harper's Weekly* published personal notes about significant people, as well as obituaries of prominent citizens who had recently passed away. In this manner the men of the garrison kept in touch with the world around them.

The post library had a collection of several hundred books by the 1880's. These volumes covered a wide variety of topics. Soldiers could read history, biography, fiction, adventure, and numerous other subjects. A book order sent by 1st Lieutenant W. T. Duggan in 1884 included the following titles, among others, and their cost:

The Campaigns of the Civil War, complete Scribners	$8.50
Van Horne's Life of Gen'l Geo. H. Thomas	2.10
Nights with Uncle Remus	1.60
Recollections of a Naval Officer by Parker	1.40
The Secret Service of the Confederate States in Europe	4.20
Anne by Miss Woolson	1.00
History of Minnesota by Neill	1.50
Alhambra and Kremlin	2.00
Les Miserables, Hugo	1.00
Henrietta Temple, Disraeli	.80
Arabian Nights	.60
Romola, George Elliot	.60
The Innocents Abroad, Mark Twain	2.00
Forty Years After, Dumas	1.00
East Lynne, Miss Wood	.50
The Lost Atlantic, Donnelly	1.34
Life of Ben Franklin, Parton	2.15

When received, these new works were made available for the garrison.

The government built a new reading room in the fort in 1879. This building also served as the post schoolhouse. Prior to this, the library had been in the rear of the post adjutant's office. The new facility made it possible for the army to provide greater educational opportunities for the garrison. Men were granted free access to the collection both mornings and evenings. They could check out any books they wanted for a week. Newspapers were not circulated until they had been in the library for at least twenty-four hours. The borrower assumed responsibility for any damage that might occur to materials charged to him. For a few years army teachers conducted classes for both the soldiers and the garrison children. Instruction sessions for the men were held in the evening with attendance strictly voluntary. In 1882-83, the number of soldiers participating ranged from seventeen in September and October to zero in June. Each man selected whatever subject he wanted to study. Some learned how to read and write better, while others studied history, mathematics, geography and other academic disciplines. Men who took part in this program believed they had benefited from their labors. Captain Edwin Sellers felt the same way, when he cited the fact that every man in his command could read and write.

Although most of the men did not have families, those who did needed a school for their children. Most of the time these youngsters attended the village school. However, there were attempts to run a school in the fort. During much of the 1880's and 1890's classes were held in the post schoolhouse from September through June. In 1883 nine children over the age of five attended, but some years there were fewer. Captain Sellers noted that during the 1882-83 school year "satisfactory progress was made in reading, writing, arithmetic, spelling, geography, grammar, history and drill (setting up, marching, and manual of arms)." If a qualified man could be found among the ranks, the post commander appointed him the post schoolteacher. Whether or not the school operated depended upon the presence of a man competent to teach.

A dispute over the village school resulted in one of the most bizarre incidents in the army's experience on Mackinac Island. In 1867, largely through the efforts of U.S. Representative Thomas W. Ferry, the United States Treasury Department and Indian Bureau leased the old Indian Dormitory to the island school board. Using this building, the board established a ten-month school year for over two hundred children. While the issue as to whether the dorm should be permanently leased to the board was still unsettled, Captain Leslie Smith took command of the fort. Paying close attention to military detail, he questioned the validity of the lease. Smith contended that, since the dorm was on War Department lands, Department approval was required for any use of the property.

He advised that the army regain possession of the structure. Smith

Post schoolhouse.

backed up his recommendations with allegations that the school children were a nuisance to the garrison. Smith also wrote to the school inspector, Dr. John Bailey (who later became the post surgeon), informing him of his position on the matter. He accused the children of "climbing over fences, hurling stones down the hill . . . and committing other depredations." The school board denied these charges and emphatically stated its intention to keep the school open in the dorm. Following a series of maneuvers Smith finally received orders to take possession of the building. On May 31, 1870 an armed detail commanded by Lieutenant Matthew Markland dismissed the pupils and locked the building. Markland left a sentry at the door to prevent any civilians from attempting to enter. Needless to say, most of the villagers were quite unhappy with Smith and the tactics he used to close down their school. Despite all of his troubles, Smith lost the battle. Several weeks later Congress passed a law turning over the property to the board of education to be used as a school for the village.

While the army made worthwhile efforts to provide for the intellectual needs of the men at Mackinac, it also attempted to provide for their religious needs. Upon the second floor of the barracks, a chapel had been built. The furniture included a pulpit, communion table, and a reading desk. The Reverend John O'Brien, an Episcopalian minister, held Sunday worship services here during most of the two decades he served at Mackinac. First appointed in 1842, he was still at the fort in 1861. He preached and served communion to interested enlisted men and officers. These ceremonies were open to the public and some of the villagers made their way up the hill each Sunday to worship. Visiting clergymen often conducted services here during the summer when no chaplain was present.

Except for O'Brien and Reverend James Knox who succeeded him for a short time in the 1860's a chaplain rarely served the garrison. As a result, any soldiers desiring to take part in religious exercises depended upon churches in the village. In June, 1820 the Reverend Jedediah Morse was on the island and held Presbyterian services on Sunday. Dr. William Beaumont attended one of these in the morning and went to a Catholic ceremony in the afternoon. Catholic soldiers found a church home at St. Anne's parish that had been on the island since 1781. Between 1823 and 1837 many of the officers and men attended services held at the Presbyterian Indian mission. Reverend William M. Ferry founded this school, and after 1826 it came under the auspices of the American Board of Commissioners for Foreign Missions. Ferry ministered to the entire island community, and his congregation, though small, included some important local figures, such as Robert Stuart and Henry Schoolcraft.

Mission Church.

During the late 1820's, Dr. Richard S. Satterlee, the post surgeon, took a very important part in the church affairs at the mission. Both he and his wife regularly participated in the services and became close friends and confidants of Ferry and his wife Amanda.

Although other officers attended church, their devotion or religious commitment was not as deep as the Ferrys wished. In 1829, Mrs. Ferry described Lieutenant Colonel Enos Cutler as "a man of the world" who went to church during good weather. With the exception of Lieutenant Lynds and his wife, who occasionally visited the church, the other officers showed little interest in church matters, coming only when they felt like it. Enlisted men who were not on duty often participated in the morning services with a few returning for the evening meetings. If the men bore arms on their way to church, they stacked them at the door before entering.

Even though many of the men were exposed to Christian teachings, the missionaries questioned the effects their work had on the soldiers' lives. Careless and reckless living seemed to indicate that these men had a greater concern for the things of the world than for the things of God. Consequently, the fruits they harvested were drunkenness, gambling, fighting, and cursing, among others. Men like Reverend Ferry demanded that a true believer of God make a total commitment to him and live a life that exemplified this relationship. Few soldiers were willing to do so. Commenting on the spiritual condition of the garrison at Mackinac, the Reverend Jeremiah Porter, while at St. Mary's, wrote that "the soldiers are going on regardless to death as the ox to the slaughter, tracts, temperance, or the Bible Class cannot enter the gates of the Fort." Despite this bleak observation, a number of the men did concern themselves with religious activities, although rarely with the fervor of a Presbyterian minister.

The commanding officer and his subalterns could do much to influence the spiritual climate of the garrison. An officer who was vile or abusive certainly set a bad example for his men. On the other hand, an officer who demonstrated saintly qualities might encourage his men to get involved in religious and church affairs. When Captain Leslie Smith took command in 1869, he wanted to offer the post chapel to visiting clergy for services. To his great dismay he discovered that the chapel had been desecrated; the furniture had been dismantled, the carpet torn out, and the other vestiges removed. Some of the officers and a non-commissioned officer had carried away the spoils to decorate their living quarters. These actions infuriated Smith, and they undermined the promotion of religious services. Attempting to establish a more favorable spiritual atmosphere, he recommended that when the church call was beat, at 10:30 each Sunday, all men go to church. At this time there was a Roman Catholic and a Methodist congregation on the island. The number of churches increased in 1882 when Trinity Episcopal Church was built.

Despite the best efforts of officers like Smith and dedicated ministers like Ferry, most of the garrison put worldly affairs and interests before spiritual concerns. In this respect the soldiers differed little from most civilians on the island. Just as they put business and pleasure before religion, so did the men at the fort. Being preoccupied with duties and secular interests, it is doubtful that many of these soldiers gave prolonged thought to theological questions. They considered the hour or two they might spend in church on Sunday morning a sufficient religious commitment. Certainly some men did apply religious teachings to their lives, but most found church doctrines incompatible with their life style.

The army and individuals in the community attempted to meet the intellectual and religious needs of the Mackinac garrison. Although the scale of this effort was not large, opportunities were accessible to the men. The post probably owned the largest library on the island having over six hundred books by 1890. By supplementing this with a number of periodicals, a supply of current information and ideas was made available. Likewise, the men were frequently encouraged to participate in various religious activities and to make spiritual commitments. Yet each man decided for himself whether or not he wanted to read books, attend classes, or go to church. Many of the temptations around him appeared to be more glamorous and enjoyable than these activities. He often opted for a card game, a billiards match, or a trip to the village.

Fort with City in back

XI.

FAMILY, HERITAGE AND COMMUNITY

Some of the officers and a few enlisted men had wives and children, but most of the soldiers were single. Although the availability of eligible young ladies was limited, the troops were able to find some female companionship on the island. Mackinac's bustling economy and strategic location attracted many businessmen and visitors throughout the nineteenth century. These men brought their families with them and formed a lively community. In addition, a number of men and women worked for the local business establishments in various capacities.

Most soldiers serving at Mackinac were immigrants. The census figures showed that in most years there was a preponderance of foreign born men with only 1880 having an equal number of native born soldiers. In 1850 the large scale Irish immigration to America was reflected at Fort Mackinac, as seventeen out of thirty-seven enlisted men were from Ireland. In 1860 German-born men formed the largest block of immigrant soldiers. Throughout the rest of the garrison's existence, the Irish and Germans were present in the greatest numbers; but they were accompanied by men from Italy, France, Canada, Scandinavia, and the British Isles. A good number of the huge waves of nineteenth-century immigrants found their way into uniform. Interestingly, most of the officers were native Americans, although several, such as Captain Leslie Smith, were born in Europe.

The ages of the soldiers ranged from seventeen to over fifty, with the exception of Ordnance Sergeant William Marshall, who was seventy-nine in 1880. Generally the average age of the enlisted men was between twenty-six and thirty-one with the officers being a few years older.

Most of the men had little opportunities for advancement beyond sergeant, and only a few made it that far. In 1880 one soldier, aged fifty-two, was still a private. Even though many of the troops were in the prime of life, their occupation was not particularly attractive or promising to a would-be wife.

A frontier military outpost was not an ideal place to raise a family. Fort Mackinac had limited quarters for non-military personnel. Enough room was available in the officers' quarters and the blockhouses for several families, but there were not accommodations for the families of fifty or sixty men. Although the influences of the men's bad habits on children may not have been any greater than in many civilian settlements, a soldier did not have the freedom to move with his family to different surroundings. He was stuck in the army until his enlistment expired. Most military families also discovered that they had little privacy. Most of the garrison quickly learned of any family problems, be it an argument, a child getting into mischief, or a scandalous rumor.

Despite these difficulties, some of the men did marry and bring up children. Some had met their wives while in the service and planned to become civilians as soon as their five-year enlistment was over. Others made the army their career and did not let this prevent them from having a family. Quite often they were non-commissioned officers. In 1850 two sergeants and two privates were living with their families. Sergeant

Children's toys and marbles found during archaeological excavations at Fort Mackinac.

94

William Marshall, who spent over twenty years at the fort, had six children. The 1860 census showed five families living in the blockhouses. Although the quarters were a bit crowded, things were not as cramped as they might have been. Fortunately Marshall and his wife, who now had eight children, were living in the ordnance sergeant's quarters. Of all the census reports, the one for 1860 showed the highest percentage of married enlisted men with seven out of fifty-nine having families. In other years, no more than five appeared as family men.

A much larger percentage of officers were family men. This was not surprising since more of them were career men, and they had more freedom and better living accommodations. The fact that the officers were higher paid enabled them to support a family and maintain a household. Many had servants who helped cook, clean, and tend to the children. Two servants helped Mrs. Henry Pratt manage the large commanding officer's house as well as her six children during the time her husband commanded the fort between 1858 and 1861. Quite often the post surgeons brought their families to Mackinac. Doctors William Beaumont, Richard Satterlee, William Alexander Hammond and others lived with their wives and children in the surgeon's quarters. Apparently, the living conditions were satisfactory, particularly for Beaumont, who commented that his family was in good health and "blessed with most of the other comforts of life, and enjoyments of this world."

Life kept the army wife busy. Many had small children who required much care and attention. Mother nursed them through illness, made many of their clothes, and prepared their food. When she was not looking after children, she did her laundry and housecleaning, and during the winter she made sure the fire was kept going. The post sutler found these women to be good customers and stocked many goods for them. Their husbands bought a variety of cloth, threads, buttons, dyes, and ribbons to be used for garments that mother made for the family. The women spent many hours sewing shirts, dresses, breeches, and coats for their children and themselves. When time and money were available, the lady of the house might put together a dress of the latest fashion to be worn at some garrison or village social function.

Fortunately life involved more than work. Some of the officers' wives escaped the routine housekeeping duties because of the labors of their servants. Their husbands, as leaders of the post, kept company with some of the prominent civilians on the island. It was not surprising that their wives also had contact with each other. Mrs. William Ferry of the Indian mission made great efforts to visit the invalid wife of Lieutenant Colonel Enos Cutler. Amanda Ferry also had other friends among the women at the fort, particularly Mrs. Richard Satterlee. Throughout the post's history the leading merchants, traders, religious leaders, and important summer cottagers socially mixed with the officers and their wives. While the men folk might gather for a poker game, the women exchanged tidbits of information about their families or new developments in fashions. Mackinac may have been isolated during much of the year, yet the women living there probably had a more active social life than many of their counterparts on frontier farms and settlements.

Both single officers and enlisted men sought the company of the island's young ladies. Unfortunately for the soldiers, there were more young men than women living in the village. Despite this discouraging situation, single women between the ages of fifteen and thirty-five comprised a significant portion of the population. Ninety-three of the island's population of 1,080 in 1860, and seventy out of 722 in 1880 were unmarried females. In addition to the sixty or seventy troops there were more than enough unmarried civilian men to keep the girls entertained. These women were daughters of island residents, servants in private homes, hotel employees, school teachers, and store clerks. The army also employed several laundresses to wash the men's clothes and bedding. Most of these young ladies married at a young age and to local men, which worked to the soldier's disadvantage.

Occasionally a romance between a soldier and a local girl resulted in marriage. When this happened, it was usually cause for a happy celebration, particularly if the man was an officer. On January 5, 1874 Lieutenant Thomas Sharp married an island girl. To commemorate the nuptials, Sharp threw a party at his own expense for his entire company. The festivities included supper and much merriment. Another ceremony took place on March 6, 1890, uniting Miss Jessie Cable to Lieutenant Benjamin C. Morse in marriage. After the wedding, they visited a Lake Superior mining town.

In some instances these romances continued for years after one of the parties had left the island. Lieutenant Dwight L. Kelton, who served at the fort during the early 1880's, became acquainted with Miss Anna L. Donnelly of Mackinac. Several years after his transfer from the garrison, they were married in Milwaukee, Wisconsin, on July 19, 1889.

Clay pipe smoked by a Mackinac soldier.

96

It was quite fitting that Kelton, who had a great love for Mackinac Island, should meet his wife at the place he held so dear.

One of the most interesting legends regarding the love life of a Mackinac soldier involved the activities of Lieutenant John C. Pemberton. As the story goes, Pemberton met the beautiful Sophia Biddle, daughter of Edward Biddle, while stationed at Detroit and fell in love with her. Before she would marry him, she insisted that John first meet her mother, who lived on Mackinac Island. After he was transferred to Mackinac, he went to visit Sophia, who was back at home, to ask her mother's permission to marry. Pemberton knocked on the door and was shocked to discover that Sophia's mother Agatha, who answered it, was an Indian woman. He left, trembling at the fact that he had courted a half-breed. Whether or not this story was true, it illustrated the interest and intrigue that often accompanied island romances.

An enlisted man sometimes learned that marriage created some very perplexing problems. For a man who had been rather shiftless or unsettled, the thought of starting a family while in the army often proved troublesome. The fact that his freedom of movement was limited might make his wife quite unhappy. If she decided that the army was not for her and wanted to leave, the soldier had to choose between her and the army. Quite often he deserted to follow his wife. Some men made the decision to leave shortly after becoming involved with a woman who promised a much happier life away from the garrison. Officers complained that a few of their men had deserted because of the influence of a harlot or a girl working at one of the hotels. Consequently army discipline and romance were sometimes in direct opposition to each other.

The pursuit of women was one of the ways the troops were drawn

An 1870 view of village from Fort Mackinac.

97

into village activities. They also became involved in the town's economic and political affairs. In short, the men of the garrison were part of a fairly complex and ever-changing community on Mackinac Island. For a settlement with a population between five hundred and one thousand throughout most of the nineteenth century, the island had a considerable amount of activity. From the 1780's to the 1830's the fur trade annually brought hundreds of traders and clerks, plus thousands of Indians to the island. After the fur trade diminished, the fishing industry employed many local people and gave Mackinac a renewed economic spirit. By the time this business was losing its importance, thousands of summer tourists were discovering the beauties of Mackinac summers. Enterprising men built several hotels, most notably the Grand Hotel in 1887, to accommodate those who desired to enjoy northern Michigan's pleasant environment. As a result, the men at Fort Mackinac benefited from the village's business and the people who passed through the Straits. More people meant there were more demands that needed to be satisfied. Consequently more shops, billiard rooms, and bars came into being which could be used by the soldiers. The many boats that docked in the harbor brought folks to the island, helping rejuvenate life in the community. After the formation of the national park, soldiers became celebrities of sorts. As visitors used the park, they encountered men in uniform and found it quite interesting to chat with them. This afforded the men an opportunity to extol the glories or miseries of military life and to learn new things about life in the outside world.

Since most of the soldiers were foreign born, they added to the mixture of races and nationalities long a part of Mackinac. In the early years the inhabitants were primarily French Canadian and British with a few blacks and many Indian visitors. After American independence, many of the French and British remained but soon found themselves competing with ambitious businessmen from the new American Republic. By 1860 the population was composed of people whose ancestry represented virtually all of the northern European nationalities. There also existed a small black population in 1860, primarily employed by the hotels. The Mission House hired Negroes as washerwomen, cooks, waiters, coachmen, porters, and laborers. Dr. William Alexander Hammond had two young blacks, Debora Davis and Isabella Fisher, working in the post hospital.

In a very integral way the soldiers found the community of Mackinac Island to be important to their lives. Just a few hundred yards down the hill existed a place where some of the men's needs would be satisfied. If they were to have contact with members of the opposite sex, they had to meet them in the village. When the prices of the sutler or post trader appeared to be too high, the soldiers might get a better bargain downtown. They found companionship and entertainment in the village saloons and pool halls. Many soldiers took part in civic celebrations and festivities, and some got religious inspiration at the local churches. For some, the village supplanted the family, at least in part.

For those with families, the benefits of the community were also apparent. Their children often attended the village school and received religious instruction at the churches. Many of the youngsters' playmates lived down the hill. The soldiers' wives found friends amongst other Mackinac women, and many times their husbands also associated with each other. The variety of goods sold in downtown shops supplemented the products available in the sutler's store or trading post. In short, the existence of the village on Mackinac Island did much to enrich the lives of the soldiers and their families while they lived at Fort Mackinac.

Even though the number of families at the fort was small, they did have an impact on the garrison. The army established a school for the children and, when possible, employed a teacher. Certainly the presence of women and children helped to create a homier atmosphere. Some of the bachelors became fast friends with some of the youngsters, spending time playing with them and telling about their great military achievements, both real and imagined. If there had been no families at Fort Mackinac, it would have been a desolate place.

FORT MACKINAC TODAY

In 1895 the United States Government turned over the grounds of Mackinac Island National Park and Fort Mackinac to the State of Michigan. This was done with the stipulation the state maintain the property as a park. In order to accomplish this, the Legislature created the Mackinac Island State Park Commission with former United States Senator Thomas W. Ferry serving as its first chairman. The Commission was given the responsibility for maintaining Michigan's first state park so that is could be used and enjoyed by the public.

One of the results of this change in ownership was the park's abandonment by the United States Army. Even though the soldiers had left the fort, the public and visitors to Mackinac Island expressed great interest in the vacated post. As early as 1915 museum exhibits were created and installed in some of the buildings, such as the officers' stone quarters. This only added to the appeal the original blockhouses, barracks, and other structures had for thousands of people.

However, maintenance and use of the post buildings created some real problems. Not the least of these was the expense of repairing and keeping up these structures. Attempts were made to raise revenue by renting the buildings. Several were remodelled into apartments to be rented. In 1934 architect Warren L. Rindge conducted a study of Fort Mackinac for the National Park Service regarding the possible restoration of the fort. His survey revealed that much work was needed on some buildings if a historical restoration project was to be undertaken.

A large scale program was not started at this time. However, during the mid-1930's considerable work was done within the fort's walls. Many

Fort Mackinac in 1972.

buildings were whitewashed and repaired. Fort Holmes, on the hill overlooking Fort Mackinac, was reconstructed. Much of this work was performed by the Civilian Conservation Corps.

The idea of restoring the fort lingered for many years and began to become a reality in 1957. At that time, the Commission decided to make a serious attempt to restore the garrison to its original condition. To finance this program, the Commission with legislative authorization sold $50,000 of revenue bonds. They also hired Dr. Eugene T. Petersen, a professional historian, to guide and direct the project. With the bond money an interpretative museum was created in the barracks building and new exihibits depicting life at Fort Mackinac were put in the officers' stone quarters. This new museum program replaced the old exhibits, but continued the tradition of having artifacts on display for the public. Within a year visitor admissions produced enough revenue to retire the bonds.

Since then the Commission has floated three more bond issues. The latest was in 1966 for one million dollars. The results of this program have been remarkable. By 1972 the barracks, post headquarters, quarter-master's storehouse, schoolhouse, three blockhouses, old hospital, and commissary had been restored. Most of these buildings and others within the fort are open to visitors.

Not all of the Commission's activities have been confined to Mackinac Island. In 1959 they began an archaeological and historical research program designed to reconstruct Fort Michilimackinac in Mackinaw City. This resulted in the opening of the partially reconstructed fort in 1960.

Reconstructed Fort Michilimackinac with Mackinac Bridge in background.

To date, the palisades, king's storehouse, St. Anne's Church, some traders' houses, commanding officer's house, barracks, and priest house have all been rebuilt on their original locations. In 1972 the Commission opened a maritime park just east of Fort Michilimackinac.

This exciting restoration program has preserved romantic Fort Mackinac atop the hill on Mackinac Island, and caused the old Fort Michilimackinac to rise from beneath the sand. Each year thousands of visitors are able to re-live some of the experiences of the French, British, and American soldiers, and citizens who made history in the area surrounding the Straits of Mackinac. The last soldier departed from Fort Mackinac almost eighty years ago, but it was not forgotten. The memories, legends, and experiences of the garrison thrill thousands of men, women, and children each year. Fort Mackinac today is living history.

APPENDIX

During the course of 115 years numerous units were garrisoned at Fort Mackinac. Although it is not possible to list all of the men who served at Mackinac, this appendix contains the names of most of the commanding officers and their units. Those who were in command for short periods of time while their commander was absent are not included. For the years prior to 1812 it is very difficult to determine with precision the American Regiments at Mackinac. The information regarding the British soldiers was gathered by Brian L. Dunnigan. Most American officers are listed by Dwight L. Kelton in *The Annals* (1882-1894).

I. British Commanders, 1780-1796

1779   Lieutenant Governor Patrick Sinclair, 1st Battalion, 84th Regiment of Foot, (Royal Highland Emigrants)

1782   Captain Daniel Robertson, 1st Battalion, 84th Regiment of Foot

1787   Captain Thomas Scott, 53rd Regiment of Foot
(Commanding officer unknown between summer, 1788 and summer, 1789)

1789   Captain John Parr, 2nd Battalion, 60th Regiment of Foot

1790   Captain Edward Charlton, 5th Regiment of Foot

1792   Captain William Doyle, 24th Regiment of Foot

1796   Lieutenant Andrew Foster, 24th Regiment of Foot

II. American Commanders, 1796-1812

1796   Major Henry Burbeck, Artillerists and Engineers

1802   Major Thomas Hunt, Artillerists and Engineers

1804   Lieutenant Colonel Jacob Kingsbury, 1st Infantry

1807   1st Lieutenant Jonathan Eastman, Artillerists

1808   Captain Louis Howard, Artillerists

1811   1st Lieutenant Porter Hanks, Artillerists

III. British Commanders, 1812-1815

1812   Captain Charles Roberts, 10th Royal Veteran Battalion

1813   Captain Richard Bullock, 41st Regiment of Foot

1814   Lieutenant Colonel Robert McDouall, Glengarry Light Infantry

IV. American Commanders, 1815-1895

1815   Colonel Anthony Butler, Riflemen

1815   Lieutenant Colonel Talbot Chambers, Riflemen and Artillery

1816   Lieutenant Colonel John McNiel, Infantry

1817   Captain Benjamin K. Pierce, 1st Artillery, 3rd Infantry

1819   Lieutenant Colonel William Lawrence, 3rd Infantry, 1st Artillery

1821   Captain Thomas C. Legate, 2nd Artillery, Company I

1823   Captain William Whistler, 3rd Infantry, Company E

1825   Captain William Hoffman, 2nd Infantry

1826   Captain Alexander R. Thompson, 2nd Infantry, Company A

1828   Major Joseph H. Vose, 5th Infantry, Companies G and H

1829   Lieutenant Colonel Enos Cutler, 5th Infantry, Companies G and H

1831   Captain R. A. McCabe, 5th Infantry, Companies A and B

1832   Major Alexander R. Thompson, 2nd Infantry, Companies A and B

1833   Major William Whistler, 2nd Infantry, Companies A and B

1834   Captain John Clitz, 2nd Infantry, Companies A and G

1836   2nd Lieutenant J. W. Anderson, 2nd Infantry, Companies A and G

(Post abandoned June 10, 1837, regarrisoned May 18, 1840, except for August and September, 1839, when Company C of the 2nd Artillery was present under the command of Captain Samuel MacKenzie)

1840   Captain Harvey Brown, 4th Artillery, Company H

1841   Captain Alexander Johnston, 5th Infantry, Companies G and I

1842   Captain Martin Scott, 5th Infantry, Companies G and I

1845   Captain Silas Casey, 2nd Infantry, Company C

1847   Captain Morgan L. Gage, 1st Regiment of Michigan Volunteers, Companies B and G

(Post abandoned from June, 1848, to November, 1848)

1848   Captain Charles H. Larnard, 4th Infantry, Company A

1852   Captain Thomas Williams, 4th Artillery, Company L

(Post abandoned from October, 1856, to May, 1857, and from August, 1857, to May, 1858)

1857   Captain Arnold Elzey, 2nd Artillery, Company E

1858   Captain Henry C. Pratt, 2nd Artillery, Company G
      (Post abandoned between April, 1861 and August, 1867, except for volunteer units)

1862   Captain Grover S. Wormer, Stanton Guards, Company A

1866   Captain Jerry N. Hill, Veteran Reserve Corp.

1867   Captain John Mitchell, 43rd Infantry, Company B

1869   Captain Leslie Smith, 1st Infantry, Company F

1874   Captain Charles J. Dickey, 22nd Infantry, Company E

1875   Major Alfred L. Hough, 22nd Infantry, Company E

1879   Captain Edwin E. Sellers, 10th Infantry, Companies C and D

1884   Captain Charles L. Davis, 10th Infantry, Companies C and D

1884   Captain George K. Brady, 23rd Infantry, Companies E and K

1886   Captain Greenleaf Goodale, 23rd Infantry, Companies E and K

1890   Major Edwin M. Coates, 19th Infantry, Companies C and D

1894   Major Clarence E. Bennett, 19th Infantry, Company C

1894   1st Lieutenant Woodbridge Geary, 19th Infantry, Company C

Interior of Fort

BIBLIOGRAPHIC ESSAY

Much information for this study of Fort Mackinac was gleaned from microfilmed copies of military records in the Army and Air Force Division of the National Archives in Washington, D.C. Much of the post correspondence is found in Record Group 98 and is supplemented by the records of the Adjutant General's Office in Record Group 94. Contained in these records are several "medical histories" of Fort Mackinac which give some very interesting data for the 1870's and 80's. For information on building plans the "Records of the Office of the Chief of Engineers," Record Group 77 are very helpful. Other useful documents are the "Post Returns" from 1816 to 1895 and the "Inspection Reports of the Office of the Inspector General, 1814-1842." A very valuable source is the "Consolidated Correspondence File on Fort Mackinac, Michigan 1819-1890" from the Records of the Quartermaster General's Office of the War Department.

British and American military correspondence is printed in the *Michigan Pioneer and Historical Collections,* 40 vols. (Lansing 1877-1929), especially Volumes 9, 10, 11, and 15. Also, selections from the *Wisconsin Historical Collections,* 31 vols. (Madison, 1855-1931) are quite useful. "The Fort Mackinac Order Book, 1796-1799" (original at West Point), Lieutenant Colonel Jacob Kingsbury's "Orderly Book 1st Regiment, Infantry, June 1804-March 1806" (Original in New York Historical Society), and Benjamin K. Pierce's "Orderly Book at Fort Mackinac, 1818-1820" (original in the Burton Historical Collection) reveal much about life at Fort Mackinac prior to 1820. The Fort Mackinac Records of the Mackinac Island State Park Commission housed in the Michigan State Archives

(Lansing) contain accounts of courts-martial and some inventories. Much can be learned about the people living on Mackinac Island including the soldiers from the "Census Reports" particularly for 1850, 1860, 1870, and 1880. The *Regulations for the Army of the United States* was revised frequently and details all of the basic procedures used by the army. Printed copies of "General Orders" issued by the Headquarters of the Army give much information regarding the army's activities.

An examination of *The Century Illustrated Monthly Magazine, Harper's Weekly: A Journal of Civilization,* and the *Detroit Free Press* give a first hand account of the periodicals read by the men at Mackinac. Frank L. Mott's *A History of American Magazines, 1741-1850* (Cambridge, 1939) and *A History of American Magazines 1865-1885* (Cambridge, 1938) contain an analysis of most of the magazines found at Fort Mackinac.

Some interesting insights and antidotes are found in letters and journals written by Protestant Missionaries who passed through or lived on Mackinac Island. Some letters authored by William M. Ferry and his wife Amanda are published in *The Journal of the Presbyterian Historical Society* (December 1947, June, 1948, and September, 1948). The "Diary of Jeremiah Porter" (original in the Chicago Historical Society) and *Eliza Chappell Porter: A Memoir* (Chicago, 1892) edited by Mary H. Porter are also quite informative regarding the spiritual and physical health of the troops during the 1820's and 30's. Another authoritative source is the "William Beaumont, M.D. (1785-1853) Manuscript Collection" (in the Washington University School of Medicine Library). Some exerpts of Beaumont's letters and journals are printed in Jesse S. Myer's *Life and Letters of Dr. William Beaumont* (St. Louis, 1939). Richard P. Hulbert, a Mackinac Island businessman, kept an interesting journal during 1887-1891 which is in the possession of the Mackinac Island Historical Society.

A number of secondary works have been written about the history of Mackinac Island. Edwin O. Wood's two volume *Historic Mackinac* (New York, 1918), and Dwight H. Kelton's *Annals of Fort Mackinac* (Detroit, 1882-1894) are quite useful. Others include Roger Andrews, *Old Fort Mackinac on the Hill of History* (Menominee, 1938); John R. Bailey, *Mackinac, Formerly Michilimackinac* (Lansing, 1899); Meade C. Williams, *Early Mackinac* (St. Louis, 1903); and J. A. VanFleet's, *Old and New Mackinac* (Ann Arbor, 1870). Also of interest are Walter Havighurst's *Three Flags at the Straits: The Forts of Mackinac* (Englewood Cliffs, 1966) and W. P. Strickland's *Old Mackinaw, or the Fortress of the Lakes and Its Surroundings* (Philadelphia, 1860).

Several publications of the Mackinac Island State Park Commission deal with important aspects of Mackinac history. Among these are George S. May's *War 1812* (1962) and *Lore of the Great Turtle: Indian*

Legends of Mackinac Retold (1970) by Dirk Gringhuis. Included in *Mackinac History,* Volume I, vignette series are "Clay Pipes: A Footnote to Mackinac's History" (1963) by Eugene T. Peterson; "Military Buttons: Long-Lost Heralds of Fort Mackinac's Past" (1965) by J. Duncan Campbell; "The Mess at Mackinac" (1964) and "John C. Pemberton: A Pennsylvania Confederate at Fort Mackinac" (1968) by George S. May. A brief account of the restoration program at the Forts of Mackinac, *The Preservation of History at Mackinac* was written by Eugene T. Petersen in 1972. He also published a pictorial history of Mackinac Island in 1972.

The results of an archaeological study done on Mackinac Island in 1965 entitled "The Custer Road Dump Site: An Exercise in Victorian Archaeology" by David S. Brose appears in *The Michigan Archaeologist,* (Volume 13, Number 2) June, 1967. A list of names on tombstones in the Fort Mackinac Cemetery appears in David A. Armour's "Fort Mackinac, Michigan Post Cemetery," *Family Trails* (Fall-Winter, 1970-71). Another article by Armour, "The Past Lives (in Peace and Quiet) at Historic Mackinac Island," is in *Early American Life* (September-October, 1970).

West Blockhouse.

INDEX

Fort with City in back

Soldiers in front of barracks.

113

Southern side of Fort

THE AUTHOR

Keith R. Widder, born in Sheboygan, Wisconsin, received his B.A. in history from Wheaton College (1965) and an M.A. in American History at the University of Wisconsin - Milwaukee in 1968. He began working for the Mackinac Island State Park Commission in 1971, and he is now Curator of History. In 1989, Widder received his Ph.D. from Michigan State University. His current research focuses on the social history, with an emphasis on the fur trade, of the western Great Lakes region between 1660 and 1840.

South Sally Port

A thirty-five foot birch bark canoe at Fort Michilimackinac.

What the American Army and Navy had been unable to do, the peace negotiations accomplished in late 1814. The Treaty of Ghent called for both Britain and the United States to restore all territory gained during the war. The disenchanted McDouall was ordered to build fortifications on nearby Drummond Island for his troops. On July 18, 1815 he unhappily relinquished Fort Mackinac to Colonel Anthony Butler and the Second U.S. Regiment of Riflemen. The British erected a new fort christened Fort Collyer on Drummond Island. Though tension between Great Britain and the United States persisted for some years and though border forts were built and garrisoned, war never again came to the Straits of Mackinac.

V.

DISCIPLINE

The army had to maintain strict discipline among its men to function effectively. If the soldiers were to fight in battle, it was essential they follow orders. Also, they had to obey their officers' commands on the drill field, as well as observe military regulations at all times. When a soldier violated the rules, he was held accountable for his actions. Guilty individuals could expect quick and harsh punishment. For every man at Fort Mackinac discipline constituted a very important part of his life.

Court-martial records indicate a wide variety of offenses. Soldiers repeatedly answered to charges of drunkenness, disobedience to orders, desertion, and stealing. Although many crimes were committed, most of the troops abided by the rules. It was not uncommon for the same soldier to be tried several times a year for being drunk or disobedient. These unfortunate souls suffered some severe chastisement for their errant ways. The types of crime committed changed little during the years, but the nature of punishment did.

Nothing contributed more to the breakdown of discipline than the excessive use of liquor. Although the army issued each man a gill of whiskey as part of his daily ration until about 1830, the military found itself incapable of limiting the amount of spirits consumed by the soldiers. Some men drank to overcome the loneliness they experienced at this isolated outpost, particularly in the winter. They were a long way from family and friends without any means to contact them. Others enjoyed the effects of alcohol and did not care how it affected their behavior, as long as they had a good time. A few men got into trouble because they did not know when to stop drinking. As a result, a soldier of strong character might find himself before a court-martial because he naively over-indulged and was unable to perform his soldierly duties. Intemperance was a problem at the fort for over one hundred years, and attempts to overcome it met with little success.

Shortly after the Americans took command of Fort Mackinac, liquor became a problem for the garrison. On September 9, 1796, nine days after their arrival, seven men were convicted of "receiving and drinking public stolen whiskey knowing it to be stolen at the time, for receiving and secreting other public property and for being drunk." They received one hundred lashes each.

Major Henry Burbeck clearly recognized the evils of alcohol and sought to limit its availability. He forbid any officer to grant permission for the soldiers to receive "ardent spirits." One exception to this rule was that any soldier who re-enlisted would be issued one gallon of spirits. Burbeck believed intemperate drinking not only harmed an individual's health, but it also undermined good discipline. In an attempt to circumscribe these restrictions, men sold some of their provisions to villagers in exchange for liquor. To combat this, Burbeck ordered that each man be examined before leaving the fort. No one was allowed to take outside the fort any part of his rations without the permission of the officer of the day. Yet, this did not prevent the men from drinking.

Men found guilty of drunken behavior received stiff corporeal punishments. Even this did not keep some individuals sober. One Alexander

Post Guardhouse.

Hamilton was found guilty of being intoxicated in the village on November 6, 1804. He received fifty lashes on his bare back and fifty lashes on his bare breech for his actions. Undaunted, Hamilton stood before two courts-martial in December on similar charges. His tender body absorbed another 125 lashes as a result.

Occasionally liquor got men into more serious trouble. In December, 1804 Private John Towman, while intoxicated, broke into a store in the village. Upon conviction he was flogged and ordered to make restitution through deductions from his pay. Eight weeks later, Towman went on another bender and abused a citizen. For this escapade fifty lashes were ordered. Within another two months he got seventy-five lashes on two occasions for being drunk while on guard and while on duty in the village. Apparently neither Hamilton nor Towman regarded a good whipping as a deterrent to debauchery.

When a man was flogged, his fellow soldiers witnessed the proceeding. The lashes were administered at the guard mounting in the morning or at parade in the evening. Following the whipping the prisoner rejoined the ranks. When non-commissioned officers were convicted of drunkenness, disorderly conduct, or dereliction of duty, they had their stripes removed before the assembled troops. Usually men did not serve more than one day in the guardhouse for these offenses. The post command administered justice speedily and decisively.

When non-commissioned officers behaved in an undisciplined manner, they set a very bad example for the men under their supervision. In 1818 a Sergeant Blanchard lost his rank upon being convicted for giving liquor to his men who were cutting wood on Bois Blanc Island. Because of the Sergeant's previous record, the post commandant restored Blanchard's stripes. Not all errant corporals and sergeants had such good fortune.

However, too often men who lost their rank were reappointed a short time later because their successors either were incompetent or were court-martialed. If this happened, their commander became quite concerned. Lieutenant Colonel William Lawrence expressed his misgivings regarding this practice. In 1819 he ordered that non-commissioned officers who were reduced in rank would not be reappointed in the future. He felt that this would instill a sense of respect and honor toward their position.

In 1812 Congress outlawed "the infliction of corporeal punishment, by stripes or lashes," but this did not mean the end of corporeal punishment. The military simply used other devices to create displeasure for convicts. For a few years after this, men were sometimes flogged with a colt or a short rope with a knotted end. In 1819 two privates spent a month in the guardhouse for disobeying orders. While there, they forfeited one-half of that month's pay, ate only bread and water, and each had a ball and chain attached to one of his legs. During the 1840's men convicted of unmilitary conduct or drunkenness carried six or eight six-pound cannon balls in knapsacks on their backs. Such a sentence might last for fifteen days, with the prisoner bearing weights every alternate two hours, both day and night.

By the late 1850's the army again disciplined errant soldiers at Fort Mackinac with the whip. Those found guilty of dissertion faced very stiff punishment. In September of 1860 Private William Henderson was found guilty of running away from the army, and his superiors dealt harshly with him. Henderson forfeited all pay due him and suffered severe bodily inflictions. In addition to receiving fifty lashes on his bare back, he had a one and one-half inch letter "D" indelibly marked under his left arm. Ten days later he had his head shaved and was drummed out of the army. After the Civil War, the whip was retired at Fort Mackinac.

Through the years more changes in punishment took place. Military courts often sentenced men to a few days or weeks in confinement at hard labor. While serving his sentence the convict usually forfeited part of his pay for that time in addition to having his rations reduced. Fines, hard labor and incarceration eventually replaced the cruel lashes of earlier times.

To adjudicate alleged violations of regulations, the post commander convened garrison courts-martial. It met in the barracks or schoolhouse and consisted of three officers chosen by the commandant. The guard brought the prisoner before the tribunal where he heard the charges and rendered his plea. If he pleaded guilty, the judges considered the plea and handed out his sentence. Generally, the defendent would plead not guilty thus necessitating further proceedings. Witnesses, supporting the charges, testified against him. Usually the arresting officer or guard provided the most damaging testimony. If the accused had any witnesses to support his plea, they were given a chance to state their knowledge regarding the charges. The man on trial then offered his side of the allegation.

Following these formalities, the court determined the guilt or innocence of the defendant. If not guilty, they released him and restored him to the ranks. If guilty, they sentenced him. They then forwarded their judgment to the commandant, with any recommendations for clemency, for his approval. He frequently set aside penalties for soldiers whose previous conduct had been good or who seemed to be genuinely repentant of their misdeed. Occasionally he reduced sentences imposed by the court. Once the punishment had been approved, it was swiftly carried out.

Generally liquor contributed to minor disturbances that were settled quickly, but this was not always true. Several soldiers celebrated Christ-

Commandant's Office.

mas, 1829 in a most dangerous fashion. Taking advantage of the holiday, they consumed enough liquor to make them quite surly. When they appeared on parade in the afternoon, the armed soldiers assaulted Lieutenant Ephraim K. Smith. Attempting to resist their bayonets, Smith drew his sword to defend himself. The mutineers quickly broke the sword and threatened Smith's life. Other soldiers, seeing the fracas, appeared ready to assist in the rebellion. Fortunately, the other officers observed the incident and saved Smith from his assailants without any blood being shed. They summoned the guard and ordered six soldiers confined in the guardhouse with three men put in irons. Apparently, Smith was not blameless in this affair as his propriety was questioned the following summer. Also, the Adjutant General granted clemency to some of the men who had received sentences of hard labor, confinement, and stoppage of pay for their part in the mutiny.

During the summer of 1862, three high ranking Confederate officials from Tennessee were held prisoner at Fort Mackinac. Pictured here are Judge Josephus Conn Guild (left) and General William G. Harding. The third man was General Washington Barrows. Courtesy – Library of Congress.

Non-commissioned officers sometimes dealt with insubordination without waiting for court-martial proceedings. In 1819 Corporal John Timberlake beat a private who had interfered with his official activities. The soldier brought charges against Timberlake, who was acquitted. As a result, the young private had to answer to charges of unsoldierly conduct and using disrespectful and insolent language. Upon conviction, the court determined that the man had received sufficient punishment from Timberlake. Two weeks later, the post commander promoted Timberlake to Sergeant.

One of the most flagrant breaches of discipline occurred in 1829 when

Private James Brown was accused of murder for shooting Corporal Hugh Flynn. This incident took place in the mess hall before fifteen witnesses. Brown claimed that the musket discharged accidently, and he was unaware that it was loaded. He was then confined in the guardhouse and later transferred to Green Bay for trial before Judge James Doty. In October eight soldiers went to Green Bay to testify. Brown was found guilty and sentenced to be hanged on November 25 on Mackinac Island. He was granted a stay of execution until the following February, pending his appeal to the President. While in jail, the Reverend William Ferry tried to convert Brown to Christianity, but he showed little interest in religion. On December 8, 1829 Territorial Governor Lewis Cass wrote to Sheriff Edward Biddle informing him that President Andrew Jackson had refused to pardon Brown. Cass instructed Biddle to carry out the sentence on the proper date, which was February 1, 1830. Reverend Ferry gave the news to Brown, who appeared to be unmoved although he still maintained his innocence. Whether or not Brown was actually hanged is uncertain, but the post return for February, 1830 listed one man from his company as either having "died" or been "executed." This entry is unusual for Fort Mackinac returns since deceased soldiers were usually accounted for by the term "dead" or "died." In any event, this incident created much citizen interest and excitement as this was to be the first execution held on the island.

As more people discovered the beauty and pleasant summer climate of Mackinac Island, many desired to spend their summers there. By the early 1890's a number of cottages had been built for that purpose. The treasures that these residences held proved a great temptation for some soldiers. Authorities arrested six men on various charges of breaking and entering, burglary, and receiving stolen goods from several cottages. Their trial, held in Mackinac County Court in 1891, resulted in the conviction of four men. Two got three-year sentences to the State Prison at Marquette while the other two received terms of eighteen and six months.

After civil authorities apprehended law breakers, they threw them in the village jail. Upon learning of the arrest of two of his men in August, 1875, Captain Charles J. Dickey visited them in the jail. He found the place in a deplorable condition. The straw mattresses on the beds were rotten and stained with blood and vomit. Also, "a damp and sickly odor" permeated the premises due to a lack of ventilation, and the heat of August aggravated the situation. Concerned about the men's well-being, Dickey complained to the sheriff, demanding that improvements be made. His requests resulted in some changes, as new bedding was acquired and the cells were cleaned up. The privates, who were serving sentences of fifteen and thirty days, spent their time in a healthier environment because of their company commander's concern for them.

Conscientious officers considered their men's future well-being after they got into trouble. Although they might extend little sympathy to those of bad character, they might help a man whose conduct and attitude indicated a good character. One such officer was Major Alfred L. Hough. Peter Gilligan, a man in his command, had been convicted of theft. For his crime, he had been sent to the Albany Penitentiary. Prior to this incident Gilligan enjoyed a fine reputation, but one night he drank too much and committed the theft. Writing to the Assistant Adjutant General in 1876, Hough expressed his belief that a lengthy confinement among hardened criminals would have a detrimental effect upon this man. He also felt that Gilligan's sentencing and removal from the island would be a warning to others in the garrison. Consequently, he recommended clemency for Gilligan. Hough thought that Gilligan had suffered enough and that any further punishment would do him more harm than good.

If drunkenness was the most chronic cause for disorderly conduct, desertion was certainly the next most difficult disciplinary problem. Men deserted in large numbers, not only from Fort Mackinac, but from army posts throughout the country. This phenomenon caused great concern for the military hierarchy, and they spent much time analyzing why men would risk severe penalties to escape from their units. At Mackinac this difficulty plagued the post command until the garrison was removed from the fort.

When soldiers deserted, the commandant expended great effort to locate them and have them returned. A General Order issued in August, 1818 put a thirty dollar reward on the heads of deserters. This practice still existed sixty-five years later. Three men left Company D, Tenth Infantry in September, 1883. Their Commander, Captain Edwin E. Sellers, believed they had boarded the steamer *City of Duluth*, heading for Chicago. Offering a thirty dollar reward for each, he alerted the Chicago Chief of Police and authorized their arrest if they should appear in that city. It was a common practice for post commanders to notify local police and sheriff officers to be on the lookout for deserters.

Men might desert individually or leave with some of their buddies. Probably the most flagrant incident occurred in 1831. A corporal and eight men of a detail that had been dispatched to Bois Blanc Island to assist in the construction of a wharf left without permission. They took with them a boat, tools, and clothing belonging to other soldiers. When this was discovered several hours later, an officer pursued them for a distance of 150 miles along the eastern shore of Lake Huron. He did not find the men or the stolen property. Lieutenant Colonel Enos Cutler, the regimental commander, blamed this act on the influence of whiskey.

During the 1880's there was a rash of desertions. Between September 1, 1882 and July 27, 1883 ten men deserted. The next year the total

Infantrymen on their way to drill field behind Fort Mackinac, about 1885.

reached seventeen. With between seventy and eighty-two men stationed at the fort, this meant that from fourteen to twenty per cent of the troops left the garrison without leave.

These alarming statistics caused much anxiety for the post commander. It forced him to analyze seriously the reasons for this situation. His thoughts give us some interesting insights into procedures and conditions that created resentment among the rank and file. Captain Sellers found a number of factors that contributed to dissatisfaction, particularly among recruits. They generally spent their first year without much money. Payment for clothing and alterations came out of their initial year's pay, leaving them very little to purchase any other goods. Many times new men from the depots were not dressed to "look like soldiers" upon their arrival at their stations. Old timers might ridicule them about their appearance, generating feelings of insecurity and shame.

Sellers emphasized the necessity for the army to enlist only men of good character. Laxness in this requirement allowed many undesirable men to infiltrate the ranks. Not only did these men make sloppy soldiers, they also had a corrosive effect upon the rest of the troops. Another shortcoming in the recruiting process was the army's failure to explain clearly what the government expected of a soldier. They often failed to stress the existence of strict discipline and the fact that each man was accountable for his actions. Along the same line, recruits performed too many non-military duties, such as cutting trees, and moving dirt. Some